Furiousity

Maudie K

BALBOA.PRESS
A DIVISION OF HAY HOUSE

Balboa Press books may be ordered through booksellers or by contacting:

Balboa Press
A Division of Hay House
1663 Liberty Drive
Bloomington, IN 47403
www.balboapress.com.au
AU TFN: 1 800 844 925 (Toll Free inside Australia)
AU Local: (02) 8310 7086 (+61 2 8310 7086 from outside Australia)

Print information available on the last page.

ISBN: 978-1-9822-9279-9 (sc)
ISBN: 978-1-9822-9280-5 (e)

Balboa Press rev. date: 11/23/2021

Contents

Introduction

In 2021, the Australian of the Year was introduced as someone who didn't stop until she was able to get the State of Tasmania to change the law that enabled victims of sexual abuse to be able to give evidence against their accusers. It was then that I realised that I had a story to tell.

I was already thinking about how I would acknowledge my father who taught me how to handle myself when it came to a family based practice of sledging that could only affect the way I saw myself and along with the abuse could destroy every bit of my own self respect. My story is about how he helped me to be strong and resilient despite not being able to hear my cry for help.

I have given sledging a different name but only in so far as it is used on growing and developing children. I have called it **cringe** talk because that is how it occurs for the listener.

Most of the **cringe** metered out was for my father but I copped it because I supported him and trusted him and it made my mother furious. That's why I want to talk about fury or **furiousity.**

Many of the adults that greet children of all ages with disparaging remarks and names think they are being funny. They don't realise that the child concerned is unable to understand motives. They don't see that a child is likely to make up stories about themselves based on what some adult says over and over again. **Cringe** is something that is never needed and should be stamped out now.

But much worse than that, the target tends to take on board the hurtful parts of those opinions and just sometimes it leads to being confused about who they should trust. That is what happened to me. If my mother had not been someone who used **cringe** to put me down or put me in my place, I could have turned to her when I was molested by a family friend. I didn't trust her to care.

I want to use my story to challenge anybody who deals with children to intervene when they hear something that will do harm to a child even if it sounds funny or clever. I want to tell everyone about my father who was always there for me and taught me that there was always a way to stand up for the target and be a serious interruption.

It's time to stop passing **furiousity** down from generation to generation. It is madness to think that it does anybody any good at all. We can intervene and show adults that speaking with love is the only way to see that a child knows that they are loved, that they are clever and that they have what they need to be happy.

Even today, I hear someone passing on the **cringe** and I feel so sad.

Surely they know that the child for whom it was intended has no way of knowing their motives which in fairness to the speaker may be only ever intended to be playful.

Scary Words

Furiousity is a scary word. It suggests an aggressive way of being or a state of mind that is angry that can affect how we speak or even when we greet someone. Is that what determines how we connect with people and is it ever likely to upset and offend the vulnerable ones? This is my story. I was inspired to write it down so that I can pass it on to the people I love and at the same time, share the story of my father who understood how harmful and destructive are words that are designed to express anger, denigrate a person, particularly a little one, or impart some spurious lesson that doesn't seem to be warranted. George would ask what if you could create a serious interruption and change the way that people relate to one another and what if that change could promote love, trust, sharing and care. Why not try?

Furiousity can be behind something that we have thought to be a giggle, a hoot, a tease and even a challenge which is single handedly the most destructive and hurtful thing we can do to future generations and even the people we love the most. **Furiousity** is often delivered with a sneer.

It can start long before a child is able to work out something like a motive. Much of the time it is just an old habit copied from someone else or remembered from the past. I was reminded of the practice when I heard a grandparent call a small child "**Our little fattie**". Why would someone want to keep planting the idea that a child had a weight problem? Can you see where that might lead?

When you were a child you must have winced when some of your family only greeted you with silly phrases designed to make a joke or even 'take the Mickey out of you'. Did you ever think about how much damage it was doing to your psyche? Did you notice that the person concerned would never be the person you felt you could turn to in a moment of need? Did you notice that they would be the last person on earth you would want to share with? They think it's funny or cute and will probably claim that they didn't mean it after all.

A person who greets a child with derision and scorn never thinks about how that young person may go on to copy them later in life. It is after all, nothing that the adult can control and one can only wonder if they realise that the child can use those words to greet other children and even go so far as to bully them. The adult may have just passed on a time bomb.

And what do we make of someone who praises aggression and violence without thinking.

Nobody who does that should ever expect that child to turn to them in a time of need. It is time to notice this behaviour and take action.

What can you do to reverse these practices and how do you make it stop without 'biting off your nose to spite your face', so to speak? Maybe you think you would have to 'have your head read' to be that silly. But maybe you need to be a little bit silly to strategically deal with someone who uses these practices without losing respect and without falling out with the person involved.

The practice of diversion and trying to make it all look like a friendly exchange is what is called for. If you do hear someone speak to a child in a way that suggests there is something wrong with them or they are not very nice, what are you going to do about it? I heard an older woman who may have been a grandmother greet a child of six or seven with the words,

"Here's little stinky pants. Can't we all smell him?"

Harmless? I don't think so. Why should she be doing that to a little child and would claim that she wants to be loved. While calling him a 'smelly monster' sucks when you realise they are supposed to interpret all of that as "you are loved" doesn't make any sense at all. It not only sucks. It stinks.

Can you imagine what children in particular, could get out of only ever hearing something like,

> **"Aren't you just the greatest thing on earth. We love you so much",** or' **"Here is our beautiful child. Come here and give me a cuddle"?**

Trash talk is the opposite and it is the trash behind it that is all that **Furiousity** after all.

There are many words in the English language that are no longer in use or have been replaced. Some have just disappeared from everyday use I suspect because they mean different things to different people. **Furiousity** is one of those words that would seem to have had so many different meanings. If you do an internet search it is likely to ask you if you mean 'ferocity'. One dictionary has two simple meanings as the state of being furious and that of being insane under Scottish law.

It's also a hard word to remember and to spell. But it is a word that can be used to describe a common but insidious practice that needs to be talked about and stamped out. It is time to make some changes to how we greet people, especially children. Those who do it badly deserve to be unmasked. Unfortunately, so many have engaged in it for much of their lives.

I believe that this is a practice taught without thinking.

Those who don't know that they practice it must be made aware that **furiousity** is in full swing. I have called it **Cringe** and constructed a **cringe** emogi. Of course '**cringe**' is a verb but I think we can safely translate this verb into a noun and use it instead of the word which means 'trash talk'.

Most of us at some time in our lives have had to deal with someone we know quite well, someone in a group or someone who is a close or distant member a family who has a habit of greeting you and saying something really hurtful and dismissive. They will come across as a bit nasty, a bit angry and a bit judgmental although you haven't a clue why. Sometimes they are being very cruel, even callous and brutal. Their manner will make you feel disempowered and instantly sad and useless. Their words may be the same old same old outbursts or something totally new and hateful. If questioned, they will claim at times that they were just being funny. Have you wondered if those confrontations were designed to give them the upper hand and make them feel superior by suggesting that you have done something wrong? Have you noticed how little respect you have for the person who just had a go at you and 'dished the dirt' so to speak?

The typical greeting may go something like this:

'Now here's something that the cat dragged in and forgot to drag out again'?

Many times I have been greeted that way by someone I desperately wanted to love me. After a while you feel that you can never expect anything different but it still hurts a lot. Have you ever tolerated hurtful words just because you thought it shouldn't be doing you much harm? Well, have I got news for you? Each time you just let it pass to the keeper, you are letting yourself down and the words may come back to haunt you. Don't think for a minute that I am promoting **furiousity.** This book is about stamping out someone's bad habit. This is about protesting in a new way. Those who use this trash talk are unlikely to be trusted and they set up a barrier which stops you from sharing your stories, your fears, your joys, your breakthroughs. The next bit of news is that if you don't stamp it out, the person who just 'dished it' out will never be able to hear you when you cry for help no matter what you share and when you need to share it. Much of the time you can change their behaviour if you just try. And it really is worth trying.

Furiousity is a sad and somewhat contrived state of almost being angry. If it's a permanent thing and you feel diminished by their words and their constant attacks, the relationship is usually stuffed. On the other hand you may just hope it is only temporary when some sort of trauma has beset your love, your friend, your relative or your workmate. Did you know that you can respond with kindness and that you can be a serious interruption and show strength at the same time and that there is a good chance that you can be a force for change or changing how it lands? Do nothing and you are a partner in **cringe**.

Furiousity can be as simple as calling a child a ***'little monster'*** or telling a young girl she is ***'acting like a tart'.*** Or it can be something out of left field like being called a '***drastic spastic'*** in jest.

It may help to know that there are many different kinds of **furiousity** as different as the people who blurt out all sorts of sayings, curses or disparaging remarks without thinking. They are all backed up by learned behaviour but how they affect you and how you deal with them will depend on whether you are caught off guard and whether or not you have been lucky enough to have had some training in recognising the anger that is there in the moment and turning it off before it really hurts. This is not about counselling or trying to get that person's head screwed on the right way. It's about taking charge with your response to what that person thoughtlessly says that seems to be designed to express their fury or disdain. This is what I learnt from George, my Dad. My dear father was the target of a very angry wife who was also my very angry mother. She was very cruel.

The fact that this practice has not been given a name so far is an indication of how little we understand the harm that it does. You may come up with something better than **Cringe** as a name.

I like the word **cringe** because it is in line with how you ought to feel when it happens to you.

What matters is that we see it as a common way of putting the audience down and a common way of greeting children in particular in some misguided sense that it is for their own good.

Children don't want to be told that they are not loved. Even if their parents are very loving and only ever say things that are both loving and helpful, when someone else marches in and tells them they are inferior and not lovable, it can destroy their self confidence and they start to wonder about themselves and who to trust.

In my opinion, **Cringe** is almost the worst thing you can do to any child apart from a brutal bashing or 'a poke in the eye with a sharp stick', so to speak. Why would you say those things if you knew it would go on hurting for such a long time?

These are some of the bad outcomes nobody acknowledges and many people ignore:

- The recipient feel s degraded and small
- There will be no trust possible between the **cringe** user and the recipient.
- The recipient will be unable to differentiate between **cringe** and discipline.
- There can be no affection between the parties
- Information sharing is not possible.
- Objectivity is never there.

That behaviour had a bad effect on my relationship with my mother. She had learnt how to confront and shame us with her disparaging comments from her mother and I suspect, her mother before her. Mostly she picked on me. Yet she told me I had to be a good example to others.

My dad George was deaf but he always knew that **cringe** was in use. I think that he must have spent his whole life studying people, interrupting and changing behaviour. Sometimes he didn't win. Mostly he did and he taught me the power in intervening and how to be a positive interruption.

I knew, all of my life that my father was there for me. Inside that silent world was unconditional love and that was why he seemed to have all the skills he needed to help me move on. He hid his deafness and not knowing that I was so very sure I could tell him all my problems and about my fears. When I was ashamed I would talk to his back, when I was sad and fearful it was best with my ear against his beating heart. Oops! Now I know that he didn't hear me I realise how important it was that he let me share and in sharing I was made free. In sharing, I could move on. And I can say right now that I never used **furiousity** on anyone. My mother? Well, that was another question.

I watched my dad deal with the manic attacks by a spouse who never knew when to stop screaming at him. He was never rude or unkind. You would have never heard him curse or swear.

George never lost his cool. He always knew exactly what he was doing and it usually worked. He taught me how to deliver a retort that was designed to be amusing and even kind. He never raised his voice in anger. He never engaged in conflict. Of course none of his off centre remarks ever modified my mother's behaviour but she did pause and for long enough. She was always angry but she was usually disarmed. My father taught me to trust that I could respond in a way that kept my dignity and stopped me from breaking down. George was never cruel or nasty.

With my mother Lillian it was clear that he could not win because she would still be angry, but George really was the winner. He never stopped loving her.

The most powerful weapon against **cringe** includes copious portions of spontaneity, frivolity, hilarity, great fun and joyful pranks. It was never about making someone feel stupid or risking making them even angrier. Never! He could slow down the rant and make those who watched the encounter dare to smile and see that justice was done. My mother's rants were much the same most of the time. She would say the same things to each of her daughters but as the eldest I always got an extra burst. It would sound something like

"Here's her ugliness come to tell us how wonderful she is."

Ouch! That hurt! Until I started to learn from George I would slink off into my bedroom and have a good cry. When I emerged, she would start in on me for avoiding one or all of my duties.

The way I usually dealt with my mother's rants was to sneak into the house after school and hide in my bedroom or the back shed until she realised that I was home. Sometimes I would have something important to share with her but it had to wait until we were not alone. Even then, she would often turn on me claiming that she was doing it to show my younger sisters and my little brother how they should behave.

I have to say that I was afraid, not of my mother, but her temper and how she would make me feel at the end of one of her tirades. George was completely different. He would greet me with a fine compliment and often tell me how proud he was of my achievements. And I believed him with all my heart. It hurt to hear her attack him but he always knew what to say and I could see how little of what she said really landed. I did notice that with me it was always being angry with me or a view of something in which she seemed to be suggesting that I was responsible. As I got older I noticed that my sisters were also being given the **cringe** treatment but she was expressing her disappointment in them saying

"I thought you would have known better"

Lillian's attacks on me would usually start with

"You never get anything right do you?"

George would always tell me not to ruffle her feathers. Sadly, I didn't quite understand what he meant until one day I told her I would leave home and she made me go and pack a bag.

I learnt to respond by saying sorry many times until she calmed down and then made some excuse that it had been a bad day.

The next thing I learned to do was to offer her a cup of tea or just say

"Got it Mum! Now what would you like me to do?"

My father always recommended being an interruption. I desperately wanted to be as clever as he was. Many years later when I started work one of my colleagues told us the story of her husband working for a new company. The three managers didn't get on at all and this is a true example of a serious interruption:

'An engineer joined a firm and was told he and his young wife were duty bound to hold a dinner party. The worry facing the hosts was how to bring together three company managers who were likely to get into some sort of squabble as the night progressed. The wives were more than happy in each other's company but the behaviour of those guys after food and drink was another matter. There was always the possibility of fisticuffs or something broken. The first two courses over, the host couple smiled at each other in sheer relief. Dessert was served and before anyone could take a mouthful, the door of the dining room was flung open and the three year-old daughter of the hosts marched into the room with her

nightgown bunched up under her armpits. She walked straight to where the three men were seated and pointing at them said, "You, you, you left the seat up and I fell in." There were no arguments and no raised voices that night and it changed the dynamics in the office from that moment on. That was a 'serious interruption'.

It changed the way those guys related to one another and if someone raised their voice, everyone would laugh. When things got a bit tense around the office someone would ask "who left the seat up?"

Isn't that just the coolest tale? I never forgot that story because it proved that stamping out aggravation and anger is good for organisations and their people. It's good for everyone and it always means success is possible. That was a serious interruption engineered by a little child.

My father George would probably have said that a serious interruption of a hilarious kind would be enough to stop *a* **cringe** *episode* dead in its tracks. As my mother greeted him with her voice raised he would say,

"Gee you've had your hair done and it looks so good"*, or,* ***"Hang on. Left something in the car"***

After a while, I realised that George always left something in the car just in case. He just came back and apologised for interrupting what she was saying. By that stage she had given up.

I lived with my mother from my mid twenties to mid thirties and I am sad to say that Mum's **furiousity** was permanent and she never knew she was the big loser. After I married and moved away she just became worse. Each time I went to see her she would greet me with one of her awful sayings. I always wondered if she used **cringe** on other people.

One of her classic greetings was

"I thought you must be dead. Oh you are aren't you?"

I would respond with something like

"Zombie's always come home Mum, that's where the action is".

I had forgotten about Dad's way of dealing with it by saying something like,

"Will someone get a hammer. I just noticed a mail worm poking its head up on the letter box. I think it's eating our correspondence."

I wish I had remembered every exact way that George was able to interrupt the barrage that greeted him. I tried my own interruptions but I never really changed Lillian's need to lash out and be cruel or dismissive. I was too late. She was too practiced. For the last ten years of her life I was the one who looked after her needs. I never really felt that she cared about me. Why me?

I was the last to marry and there was nobody else available to keep her company. What I did do was soften the blow for myself and much of the time I could avoid being left hurt and so sad.

It's time to talk about **Cringe**.

If I was declaring it a noun **cringe** is a word that sums up all of the bad feelings that come from someone who is about to shell out a reasonable dose of **furiousity**. When somebody greets you with disparaging remarks and makes you feel sad and bad, that's pure **cringe. Cringe** can disable and disarm. It has no value whatsoever and it is time that it was met with a serious interruption.

A serious interruption would mean that we can maintain relationships, treat people with respect and above changed the behaviour of those people who seem to take pleasure in treating us badly.

I never stopped the **cringe** greetings that came from my mother although there were times that I felt she waited for some response from me. I would just stay quiet.

My mother would always take the opportunity to put me in my place and tell me that I was not up to scratch. She was a **cringe** expert. I didn't trust her. She died aged 97 and quite alone

Today is a day full of confusion and doubt. Have I done the wrong thing? Why did I leave her to die alone? It's too late to go back. Maybe I should have stayed. I can't go back now. It's done. Will I regret this later or will I know it was what I had to do to stay safe? They (the nurses) offered me a bed close by so that I could be with her when she took her last breath but an hour ago I just put my bag in the car and headed for home. I do know what it's like to have been with someone who was dying and I didn't really want her to show me love with her dying eyes or tell me she actually cares about me at the end. Maybe then I would have heard myself telling her that I don't want her to go. In the nursing home she is not a burden on any of us but she is old and weak and frail and still furious. She has always been furious. Some may just see her as very sad and angry but to me she is just furious about her life and being alive and of course she will be that way until the very end and frankly, that's her problem and I don't care.

This is from my diary 4 *September 2013*

I don't know if my mother was angry when she died. I left her that night because I didn't want to see her leave this life still being angry with everyone around her and still, have to wonder why she was still so very angry with me. I didn't want to hear her say something hurtful ever again. Later I found a note in her address book that said "I love you the most."

Furiousity it seems is a word that not only described the individual who was about to turn a greeting into a confrontation, it describes the practice of disarming the audience and keeping some control. The words used will change from subject to subject and on each different occasion.

A lot of the culprits think that what they are saying is funny and that just shows that they haven't thought about how it lands. By calling it **Cringe** you will know that it is something revolting and hurtful. A dead giveaway is the wince. After a time, children learn how to snuffle the wince replacing it with a look of defiance. This has the effect of making the person dishing out the **cringe** think they are making a point.

When will they acknowledge that the child is probably very close to tears? I have watched them hide behind another adult.

Often the words are too harsh. One example of this is the decision to call a small child ***'a monster'***. Children hear about monsters and see pictures of them on the TV and somehow they are expected to tone down the way that they receive and process the description coming from Dad or Mum, Uncle or Aunt, Nana or Pa, Sister of Brother. No child can be that much of a monster. And then we wonder why they turn into monsters don't we?

But now the words like ***'monster'*** became so well used and so often used to keep control and others like my angry dying mother that those who uttered them were no longer capable of being happy about anything even as she faced her maker. I was called a 'little tart' from a very early age. At first I thought I was be likened to a jam tart. Somehow I found out what a tart was and although I didn't completely understand it you will see from parts of my story that are told in the pages that follow, it made me feel ashamed and very bad indeed.

The Meaning Of Anger

AS SUGGESTED, **FURIOUSITY** IS NOT USED IN GENERAL CONVERSATION. But it is a neat word to describe a practice that seems to have been there for generations. Other words that may be used are 'anger, nastiness, bitchiness, cruelty, vindictiveness and all sorts of words that describe the ability to slag off, put down, demean and insult. The people who use this approach don't realise that this is what is happening. It is high time they did.

How many times did the label **'trollop'** get used in a greeting to a ten year old or younger? There are so many reasons why it has to stop. How many lives might be changed if the protagonists were unmasked and if the ones who were treated so badly knew how to change their behaviour? Many times, my supposedly loving mother said that I was called Maud because I was "**MUD with an A**."

Let's explore the two meanings listed for this nearly dead word, '**furiousity**' as firstly, the state of being furious and the other in Scottish history referring to the state of being insane.

My mother Lillian would never been considered insane. She was insanely furious to the end and I will always wonder if she ever really felt anything for her children because I saw no evidence of unconditional love and understanding. She was always disappointed in us. I don't know why. And I never trusted her. I never could tell her about my worries or my problems. The way that she greeted me with some hurtful remark told me that I could never trust her to show me any sympathy, understanding, respect or consideration. Why would I trust her? Why did she feel that she had to be so dismissive and cruel with us in order to keep control? Did it make her feel good?

She didn't seem to mind that we couldn't find a way to relate to her with anything but suspicion? I wanted to say "don't you want us to love you"? I was always afraid of the response. Even when I was being nice to her I was sure she would probably turn on me. I do remember that I would walk into the kitchen with my sisters and brother and I would be the only one she would direct her nasty greeting to. When I asked her why she said that it was because I was the eldest and I should set the example. None of that made sense.

I can't imagine why she would have given birth only to not need her children and then to turn on them to punish them whenever she could. I can't imagine how someone would lose two of them to an early death and still be so angry with them for their ingratitude and for leaving without permission. And I don't understand why a mother wanted the rest of us to join her in seeing their passing as a reason for anger rather than loss.

How often do we ever hear someone say that they inherited a mother or father's bad temper, intolerance, negativity and suspicion of other people? We might talk about looks, ability to swing a cricket bat, dress sense, food intolerances, maladies, prejudices and religious preferences but we never usually refer to general demeanor displayed by our elders before us or wonder if what we just said will hang around to affect that person in the future. Conversely, we may refer to our responses as a tendency to be 'grumpy' as a general rule or 'mean spirited' about certain topics or people.

Some would argue that the tendency to rely on **furiousity** is inherited along with eye colour and straight hair. But what if it was only a learned response to signals that a parent or grandparent was able to send unfettered to a young mind who then, without a contrary view, is forced to accept that it is how life is and how it needs to be approached for survival and even success?

How important would the first informative days, months, years of a life be in establishing the power of that person to deal with the choices, upsets, conflicts and major decisions that life will deal out to them? I have heard my sisters say things just like their mother did.

There was a period of 10 years when I didn't ever speak to my mother. Then she reached out for my help and I found it relatively easy to be a serious interruption. She didn't stop her cruel outbursts and they could be something like

"If I knew you were coming I would have found a big stick."

If I thought quickly I would leave the room saying I would go look for two sticks so we could fight for real. Most of the time I resisted but I was hurt nevertheless.

While she tried to think of something else to say I would have change the subject like

"I thought you would want to know I saw Helen who lived across the road in Caulfield. You know the one with the ginger cat. Her husband ran away with the lady at the cake shop. I didn't ask her if he took the cat."

It was hard work but it worked when I wasn't tired or tired and angry. I did get rather good at it.

I don't remember all of Lillian's outbursts or the cruel things that she said to our father. I closed my ears to the screaming. It was better to have left the room. I do know that she always yelled. I always thought that he must have heard her. I would watch his face and see something I thought was pity and certainly always was love. Of course, it was always going to be the case that my sisters chose to copy Lillian. It was not her words they copied but the sentiment. You will notice that if one person always talks to others in that way the nasty greeting becomes the norm.

Sometimes the person that is doing the **cringe** stuff thinks they are being funny but they are not aware of the other person's feelings and any bad things that might have happened to them.

And the tendency to deliver **cringe** never really leaves some people, ever.

Here is another example of **furiousity** or **cringe** that didn't come from my mother:

Marian has been a widow for ten years. She is alone in the world except for her sister who has a large family and a busy life. Marian catches up with a male friend from her working days via social media and starts going out to concerts and on the occasional dinner date with the man. She decides that she really likes this person who obviously likes her so she takes the opportunity to tell sister Vera that she has a new friend. Vera says,

"Is he after your money?"

At that moment Marian is diminished and her good news is turned back on her. But worse than that was how Marian had hidden the story of an Internet dating event that went wrong when the man involved was able to steal money from a very naïve participant. Vera's response to her sister's news is learned behaviour. She could have told her how happy she was for the news. What she knew to do was to make a snide and rather cruel comment. That makes my skin crawl? That's because it is such a sad case of **furiousity** based on nothing but ignorance.

The word might be dead but the practice is very much alive. What Vera did was cruel and hurtful but she was well schooled in the practice by one of her parents who liked to argue that it was good to crack a bit of a joke and take others 'down a peg or two'. Because it is **cringe** talk there is no need to ask if this is about jealousy or the need to be cruel.

Lillian would say things like,

"Don't have too much to drink. They'll ask you to take your panties off."

Why did she have to speak to me as though I couldn't look after myself? It really hurt.

It took me half a lifetime to learn how to prepare an answer for whatever she said and wherever she said it. After many years I found it easy to be nasty. That's not me.

It has taken me such a long time to realise that my father taught me to deal with the **furiousity,** the practice I now call **'cringe'** that turned up throughout my life and it's time to remind others about how it starts, how it is nurtured and why it is spread and look at some fun ways of dealing with it.

Cringe covers a whole lot of unforgiveable, antisocial, nasty, hurtful, habitual, cruel, sad, diminishing and destructive ideas and attitudes towards other people whether they are family, friends and acquaintances or complete strangers.

Cringe outbursts are propped up with constant use of stereotypes, prejudice, assumptions and conclusions we really have no right to jump to. Has anyone ever considered whether calling a child a '***monster***' actually determines how that child will behave in the future?

The use of **furiousity** or **cringe** can impact on so many areas of life only because it sets up so many impressions in the mind of the young and formulates so many ideas as it is delivered day after day be those who really should know better. Sometimes it comes from their parents and acquaintances. Sometimes it is something they made up because they were mad at someone or had some particular opinion that was a bit left field.

What you will read about here is my story. Most children would never have faced what I faced as a small child. Most children would never had experience with **cringe** that seemed to be sending all the wrong messages and confirming all the wrong ideas about what was happening while they were being molested by a family acquaintance. I can only tell my story and I am telling it for all the children who are left without a voice. This is also a story about a brave man who was wise and generous with his love and affection. His story is told because he was my hero.

George would never have uttered a cruel and hurtful word and he had, without knowing it, the happy knack of intervening whenever **furiousity/cringe** was in play.

A Serious Interruption

My father was a self educated wise man. I honour my father because I believe he was the king of serious interruptions and most of all he taught me how to deal with my mother's need to abuse and shame. George didn't just show us how to deal with **cringe**, he showed up how to think on our feet so that we would never be lost for words.

Looking back, I can see that George was trying to interrupt Lillian as she started with one of her rants as we sat down to enjoy a meal. What he started as soon as she raised her voice and it was obvious that she had some sort of a message to deliver in anger, turned out to be fun for everyone but Lillian.

Picture this! Mother and father and four children ages approximately 6 to 12 years at the dinner table. Suddenly father says,

"I saw three of them today. One was lying in the gutter with a big smile on its face. The others saw me and ran up a tree."

By this stage, everyone but Lillian was ready for the game. Of course we made it up as we went along and our mother was completely bewildered until she realised that we were playing a game. Much of the time she didn't see that we were making up a story. George was teaching us to think quickly and respond to her outbursts. Suddenly we were in control.

The other thing that he was concentrating on was how to recognise her **cringe** moments and act. You might recognise a **cringe** event because you have heard it before or something like it. Sometimes you have to make up an interruption on the run and it was easy to be even a little bit nasty or cruel. That will never help. Dad's word games and storytelling dinnertime workshops were designed to show us the power of words rather than feelings in intervening. I can only say how much it meant to me and how it helped me cope with our mother's **cringe** outbursts.

I took sick at school one day soon after I started menstruating. My mother was called to take me home. We went home on the tram and all the way home she kept asking me and loudly why I decided to ruin her day. I was hurt and confused.

"Why is it that you always seem to get into trouble at my expense?"

Most of the time we let the words go through to the keeper because their origin is unquestioned and nobody seems to ever have to justify the use of greetings and approaches to other people that were probably born out of someone's fury way back when and only serve to hurt and diminish the other person. It's time to stop the practice.

As suggested earlier, **Furiousity** or **cringe** is behind racism, prejudice, intolerance and rejection and they are all allowed because someone taught them that this was a way to relate to others with flippant comment and derision and using these comments it seems they were unlikely to be labelled as being bigots and racists.

Why is one person racist and another unlikely to ever say things that will upset other people? It's because **furiousity** is in play and even celebrated. The person who thinks they can say cruel and demeaning things about another person, a group or a way of life, is just using the same old same old method of claiming that they are so much better. Most of the time, the comments are not based on any real facts about the other person. This is how Vera spoke in **cringe** and it ended up as a bad case of racism and prejudice. Whenever Vera was challenged about her tendency to be racist she would always have the same story which really didn't support her case at all. She would continue using it as if it was gospel even though most people would discount her reasons.

Vera had told Marian that they were perfectly justified in saying that our first nation peoples got just what they deserved because her husband Kevin had been driving a semi up in Darwin when he claims he saw a drunken aboriginal woman propped up against a tree. You would have expected that Kevin must have stopped his vehicle and walked across to the woman to be sure she was under the influence of alcohol and not just napping or even dead. He didn't. It was at a bus stop. It would never occur to Kevin that the woman may just have come off a long shift as an orderly at the nearby hospital and was having a nap before the bus came.

Vera used that story to defend always coming up with the quip

"If only they could stop them drinking."
"Kevin only ever sees drunks up there."

Vera would never admit that both she and Kevin were being racist. She felt she was justified in passing the story on even though it was based on a falsehood. As suggested, these falsehoods are behind so much racism, sexism, bigotry and prejudice of all kinds.

The world is full of furious people who have no right to say that someone is doing the wrong thing by them, by society, by the world and by history.

What makes a furious person? It may surprise you to know that the main ingredient and the very first successful approach to life they seem to gain is self righteousness. Self righteousness saves you from ever being wrong, sounding wrong and being labelled as 'wrong'. The righteous sit on very high horses and as long as they remain furious they are unlikely to fall off. I always knew that Lillian wasn't feeling so hot when she addressed me as 'misery guts'. I never really knew what that mean but I did know it was pretty dreadful.

If I had accused my mother of saying hurtful things that made me feel inferior and even squalid she would say it never happened. She only did that while I was growing up and that was when she could get away with it. She enjoyed making references to bedwetting. So embarrassing!

As Lillian got older she became aware that bedwetting as a problem for senior citizens and I noticed that she stopped saying those things. Of course I was always waiting to hear them again.

Lillian died after her 97th birthday having decided to cut down on fluid so the issue was taboo and she would never be accused of raising the subject and drawing attention to her failings. By that stage she had stopped with her old comments about me but just as I was feeling less harassed she discovered two more. One was a general put down that I was

"You are much too clever for your own good"
"You always have to add your six-penneth because you don't have much to fill up your days."

Lillian always seemed to know which greetings would hurt the most. I would always say to her

"Why can't you ever say anything nice Mum?"

Sometimes I would look at the other person if there was anyone else present and see clearly that they knew what was happening. Lillian didn't notice their discomfort.

I can't remember how old I was when I was first confronted by what I now know as inherited **furiousity** in my family. I only know that before I saw that it was my inheritance I was sure that I was causing it and at one stage, feeling responsible, I was sure I must be adopted. Each time I thought like that someone would remind me how much I looked like my mother. My mother claimed it was always my father's fault. No! I could see that my father was sad but never angry.

My mother's anger was always defended with righteousness. As I grew older I noticed that fury and righteousness could end up looking almost like insanity. The Scots did get it right after all. Righteousness in the wrong hands would seem to be a deadly weapon. Every good day, every good experience and every good feedback would seem to end in misery and I was always in trouble and the reason would usually escape me. Sometimes it was the behaviour of another child and I would be blamed for not setting a good example.

Sometimes it would be for a knowing look or a smirk as I watched one of my sisters or my brother getting into trouble. Maybe it wasn't punishment. Maybe it was more about warnings, judgment and scorn. I take that back. There were the ritual beatings around the shins or ankles with a belt and its painful buckle.

I learned to keep secrets about my achievements in case they met the criteria for a dressing down and discouragement. My life was about so many secrets because I was so afraid that anything I did would get me into trouble. I could go from a bad example to Goody Two Shoes and back again in a flash.

As an innocent child I would seek and find praise only to find myself chastised and scorned for being too clever for my own good. The banter was constant and would sound like

"Just look at her. Who does she think she is? Why can't you set a good example for your sisters? There is no good coming to you my girl. Why do you think you are smarter than all of us?"

I can't remember how old I was when I decided that some people in my life were always super critical and ready to look down on and reject people who weren't "***the full quid***" as my Dad would say. George never used that term to describe anyone in particular but I knew that he had a list and he said that the people who were super critical of others were '***six stale sandwiches short of a picnic***', He also called them '***dingbats***' but he acquainted those people who were mad with righteousness and with the ones who he said were '***not up to scratch***' themselves and who had no right to judge others. This came from the most criticized and maligned man I knew.

George taught me to be kind but it wasn't just kindness and humility I learned from my father. It was resilience, survival and strength. Invented resilience meant that I could draw on tolerance and the permission to defend others and speak out about prejudice and the hurt that was being dished out to the ones who were being treated so badly. If George could forgive the way he was treated why couldn't Lillian? He would greet you with a smile and reach out to hug you. Lillian Never would.

I really craved mother to child affection. Lillian was never a hugger or someone who smiled for that matter. I used to call her '***misery guts***' without a clue as to what that actually meant. I can remember only one occasion when my mother was not angry with me. I remember that red and white check dress that she made without me asking for it and the exact occasion when I stood at the front gate looking like Dorothy from the Wizard of Oz waiting to be taken to a dance by the boy who lived across the road.

I was very proud of how I looked and the pretty dress I was wearing. I was 12 years old and I could see from the look on her face that Lillian in that moment was no longer angry with her eldest daughter. And what was more important was the closeness I felt for a very short time indeed.

I was afraid I would blink and it would go away. I did blink and it never really appeared again. That was a moment when she was no longer furious and the one time in those early years that I remember her with affection. That cold and mean lady who ruled our house cared about me for a very short time anyway. Sadly, I will never really know how she felt about me at any age.

It was only through my friendship with the neighbours that I saw that my mother just relied on her own prejudices to say quite nasty things about the people she didn't really know. I always wished she would make friends with others in our street but she just preferred to talk about them as though she knew them well. I wondered how many of them heard her yelling at George. I could hear her from out in the shed. I think people avoided her. Maybe she was lying low.

Prejudice as social status thing wasn't new to me because I saw how the man who lived up the street who would be seen each afternoon rolling and stumbling slowly home from who knows where only to be referred to as the '**neighbourhood piss pot**'. My mother said he was "**dead drunk again**" but I knew he was suffering from a fall from a horse he was training many years before at the nearby Caulfield racecourse. She knew it too. I heard that he was too proud to admit defeat and refused to spend the rest of his life in a wheelchair. That poor man! I thought he was nice.

He claimed that he would not have been able to navigate the rocks in the laneway at the top of the street and I knew he didn't drink booze of any kind. Lillian conveniently forgot the rest of his story. That's when **furiousity** takes over and nobody is loyal to anyone else. I couldn't forget that he wasn't drunk. He was just injured. I couldn't understand why my mother was finding it easy to tell lies about him and whether that meant that she told lies about everything. That was a constant worry for me. She told lies about

George and I wondered if she was telling lies about me. I didn't trust her at all.

Sometimes I would stop to chat to the man at the top of the lane him only to be scolded by my mother who said that he was not to be trusted. I knew he could never move fast enough to catch me. He often would apologise for being a nuisance and taking up too much of the pavement. Besides, he was Lynette Tilley's dad, Bill and he loved to laugh. I tried to tell Mum that he was someone's dad but she just kept muttering that ***"people like that one should be kept off the street or even put to sleep"***. I would mutter back just low enough so that she couldn't hear me whisper, ***"You too"***. That always made me feel worse.

I was very confused. How could such a nice man be a bad man? I tried very hard to dislike him.

Lynette was a year ahead of me at school. We had lived in a house in the suburb called Glen Iris when I started school as a five year-old and was sent home after a week or so because I cried too much. Lynette was at the new school I would later attend in Caulfield and because she was bigger and older I decided to be her friend so that she would happily give me some of her courage. I thought I couldn't handle what I now appreciate was imagined bullying from other kids who were taller than me and bossier and knew how to make me cry. I know I should have hated most boys and most men but I had a father that I was so very sure was nicer than the Wizard of Oz. That film made me cry because my Dad George was the Wizard, the Lion and the Tin Man all rolled up in one.

Lillian would tell me that I was a born 'sook' and that would mean she could call me ***'Sookie Baby'***. I remember looking in prams and counting the number of babies that were crying. Very few! I would walk home from school and as I passed the houses wonder how many criers lived there.

Lynette's dad had been badly injured but I never saw him crying. And Lynette never cried as far as I knew. I never actually saw Dad cry but sometimes I fancied that I heard sobbing as I walked towards the shed where he spent much of his time. It would have been after one of Lillian's 'deserved abuse' sessions. She yelled at him regularly but I never heard him raise his voice in anger.

What I loved about Lynette was the way that she would always find the right words to stop the bullies and I would be something like ***"Hello handsome!"*** The person in question would suddenly become the centre of attention and she would walk away with a big grin. I didn't know that I had to say something that worked for me and most of my attempts fell on deaf ears or I heard myself being nasty when my mother said those awful things to me.

But I listened to what George said to her and tried to learn from his example. Trying to make sense of what she was saying was useless. Most of the time it was the same-old same-old and a little more hurtful and a little more vindictive.

When I think about it now I can see why George would have been so unhappy in his perfectly silent world being screamed at by his perfectly manic wife who would always begin a tirade with

"***I know you can hear me George***".

After a while I saw that he tried to copy her but it didn't work and she would become more and more furious. Another trick that didn't work was to say

"***Speak up.***"

What did work for Dad was to say

"***Got that my lovely.***"

He told me that his inventive responses stopped him from being angry and it was better to find the words to use as a defence than to stop loving her. He was so good at it that it was easy to forget he couldn't hear. The only time he didn't respond was when she said he was a ***'coward'***.

The word had become very fashionable and was used to denigrate anybody who was male and not overseas and serving in the war. To hear it said about my Dad was so distressing. He was not one of those people I had expected to be called that. To my mind, he was brave and strong and reliable and truthful and a good man. Why would my mother call him a coward? I remember asking her why other men in our family didn't get called 'cowards'. Her answer was that my father was different.

At the end of World War Two it wasn't at all unusual to stand beside someone nursing their war wounds or walk behind someone missing a limb and walking with crutches. It wasn't unusual to see someone wince and quickly look away. Many injuries were totally hidden. I was so pleased that George, my precious Dad, had not been to war but it never occurred to me that my good fortune came about because he had a disability you couldn't see. He had never told us that he had been rejected when he tried to sign up as a soldier. I was just glad I would find him in his shed after he arrived home from work and then I would know they had not taken him today and I would still have him tomorrow. He never complained about the remarks that people made about him being a coward and the white feathers in the letterbox. George was my hero because he was strong and he didn't ever turn on me. He would help wipe away my tears. He seemed to always be on my side. I thought that George understood everything and knew everything. I was sure he did understand a huge amount about what upset me. He went to work in a factory that made army vehicles, or so I thought.

I thought they must be tanks or maybe guns so I was sure my Dad was involved in the war somehow coming home to us each night. He was somebody I could share everything with. It seemed that he was always ready to listen. I think it was actually water tanks.

I think I was a pimply teen when I realised that sweet, gentle, loving George was profoundly deaf. It was only then that I wondered how many of the secrets I had shared with him had fallen on those deaf ears while I helped him in the garden or sat with him while he watched his precious hens foraging around in the pen he had constructed beside the back lane and next to the garage.

The garage was where he did his best 'tinkering', a word my mother used to signify that he was wasting time. It was also where he would have preferred that he kept his pride and joy safe. It was an old but very much loved Studebaker that sat in front of the house with its rotor button disabled protecting it from car thieves. He had a habit of losing the rotor button and the car wouldn't start and that made Lillian worse than mad. Once again, it was her insinuation that dad was a time waster that made the whole 'no room in the garage' argument keep raising its nasty and spiteful head.

What he did have in abundance was quite a lot of 'bluff'. It was George that was always saying

"I have everything I need and so do you".

He also had a hearing aid which sometimes whistled loudly but he would always have it on hand for those times when he had to pass a test. Most of the time, 'Old Whistler' stayed quietly in his pocket probably minus its battery. I would often see him put his hearing aid in his pocket soon after he left the house. Things my mother said about my father just didn't fit. I trusted him completely.

On Saturdays, George would disappear for the afternoon and I later found out that he would attend a matinee at one of the theatres in Malvern close to where we lived. I thought he must be attending a western or a war film but it would be a drama of some kind where he could sharpen up his lip reading skills. I didn't know anything about lip readers. I didn't really know anything about deafness. I didn't know he couldn't hear music. Mum had her ballroom dancing outing and Dad had his movies. That seemed fair enough. Thinking about it now I realise that they had little in common. I suppose if you have no common ground it is much easier for one of you to be in **cringe** mode all of the time. And I had at times secretly wondered if he was pretending not to hear to annoy her.

Mum criticized Dad for everything he did anyway so why was it that so surprising? I wondered if all wives yelled at their husbands for smelling like a mechanic's shop, never paying attention, not caring too much about the family, spending money on going to the pictures.

And there were always complaints about his reading and an occasional magazine that we enjoyed reading together. Worst of all, he was not punishing us kids enough and most of all, he was not listening.

Secrets shared

It was on one of our 'happy chats' in the chook house or down in the back shed that I plucked up courage and I tried to tell my dad that I was unhappy and sad but he had his back to me when I told him that I had been molested by an uncle. Did he hear anything I had said?

I was waiting for him to be angry with me. I didn't want to see his face. He just went on hammering a nail into a piece of wood. Maybe he wasn't really deaf. Maybe Mum was right when she accused him of 'not listening' to anything she said. I thought he had heard what I said when he turned to me and said,

"You have everything you need".

I think I was about 6 years old when the molestation began but I was older when I told Dad.

In case it hasn't been made clear so far I need to say that George didn't know how to teach me anything other than tolerance and acceptance. He didn't have to teach me how to use those things. I had his good example to get me through. It didn't help with the molestation issue because I was too young to know what was right and what was wrong. He heard nothing but I heard acceptance.

What I couldn't understand was how I could go on having that horrible uncle doing horrible things to me without telling everyone that he was a monster. I took all of that to mean that I had to put up with it. George never ever told me to grin and bear it but that's what I thought I had to do.

I really hoped he wouldn't say I needed a deadly weapon to rid myself of that nasty monster. I had turned into a schemer constantly looking for a way out of going once a month to the other side of town to have dinner with people I didn't like. I tried the "don't feel well" and even thought about painting spots on my body. Nothing worked. I kept looking for clues. I kept wanting to find a solution so that I wouldn't have to keep hating Sundays, the Jerk family and cold meat and salad. Most of all I was looking for a way to stop hating myself.

I told George about my anger and self disgust but it was always behind his back. I never ever wondered if my Dad heard me when his hearing aid was whistling in his pocket.

It had all been such a shock to me. Each time it happened I would want to go and hide in a cupboard or go out and sit in the car but I was always led back into a room full of people who looked at me as though I must have been on some special outing. I would bite my lip and wait until I could go to the toilet to have a little cry. I was so helpless and so lost. Did this happen to lots of girls or only the oldest in the family? Or was it just because I happened to be clever and princess-like? I didn't know how to stop being that way.

I am now horrified that I had decided that maybe when she was old enough I could palm horrible uncle off on my sister who was eighteen months younger than me. I would wait and plan my exit. Perhaps I could find a way to outsmart the monster. I could find no words to use to stop him.

I was too small to hurt him. I didn't feel I could tell Mum. Is that what George meant? I knew he would never say anything to hurt me. In the meantime I would continue to pray and ask God to deal with my tormentor. I would just take time to succeed in getting him to die. In the midst of all those evil thoughts I would whimper, "***Gentle Jesus meek and mild***". I couldn't say the rest.

This was an ill informed world without television which arrived in 1956 with the Olympic Games. There was no media to teach us about sex and the word 'paedophile' was never mentioned by anyone. We learned about war and British history and nothing at all about growing up. Of course we had Sunday school and we had classes in bible study which were never going to mention anything about the male anatomy and say what was right or wrong about what was happening to me twelve times a year without fail.

I hated with a passion all talk of '***the fourth Sunday in the month'***. It takes over and the second Wednesday or the fourth Tuesday are also best not mentioned because they remind you that there is going to be the 4th Sunday.

And of course, impending doom is not good for a young mind. It's like being frozen in time by something that hasn't happened yet but most certainly will. It's such a cruel way to manage a little girl's life. Lillian thrived on first Fridays and all the other ways to manage her time. That was her life and a time when women had no other career except home duties something like ballroom dancing on the calendar gave her comfort.

Did she know what it did to me? It wouldn't have mattered. It was more important that she had her precious dance partner and that she could get to see him again each month. I am sure that her blindness was caused by her rage to live while dancing. I know now that Lillian didn't ever see what she didn't want to see and I couldn't have possibly known that at the time.

I was too young to work out things like motive. I certainly could never have known that what was being done to me was in the realm of most criminal. By this stage I had decided that Jesus was busy somewhere else and just didn't care too much and I was always going to be alone.

Worst of all I had a story I dared not tell. It's also a story of guilt and the ignorance of those who watched at a distance and did nothing at all or chose not to stir the pot and get someone into trouble.

I only whispered about the monster to my Dad but of course he never heard a word I had said. Was I scared of what he might do and was that why I didn't try harder? Or, was I a little afraid that all men did what the monster did and that he would tell me to be quiet because that was what all men do even to their own children. Looking back, which I do often without a lot of clarity, I realise that knowing who you are is inextricably wound up with knowing who you are not.

I didn't know if I was that '***trollop***' that my nasty nana would see in front of her. I tried to picture a 'trollop' but nobody came to mind. And what on earth was showing on the outside to let them see what I was hiding on the inside? One day someone told me that a trollop was someone who didn't wear panties. That was me when I was stuck with Uncle Jerk. It seemed that my grandmother had some insider information on my dilemma. Did she also know how desperately I wanted the smelly molester to die and preferably in agony?

The guilt was with me because I knew deep down that it was possible that I was a very bad person who wanted a grotesque death for another human being who some other person or family must love. When I realised that what I was seeking was horrible I prayed that my tormentor would just go to sleep forever.

I was comprehensively brain washed about the need to keep a secret and as I failed to tell anyone other than George the opportunity to blurt it all out came when I was just nine years old. Lillian had just told me the news that I was free at last. I had arrived home from school and found my mother sobbing her heart out at the dining room table. I reached out to comfort her not quite knowing how to and what to say. She looked up at me and then she told me that Uncle

Jerk was dead. My response was immediate. ***"Good",*** I said. Lillian's response was fast and violent. She lashed out at me using the back of her hand with so much force that I was thrown against the fire place. Her fury really stopped me from blurting out my story especially to someone like her or to other adults in the family. I don't know how old I was when I realised that Lillian was nuts about Jerk and even if she had known it wouldn't have really mattered at all.

She would never have wanted to believe ill of the man or see him as a deviant who used the mother to get to the child or in this case, the daughters. I was so sure that my father would never treat any child like Uncle Jerk had but I was not sure about the rest of the uncles.

I would avoid being hugged or touched by any of the males in the family or who were family friends we called 'uncle'. I would always wonder which of the other children, including cousins, were princesses for grubby monsters to fondle and make into trollops.

A cousin took on the job of babysitting and showed us his willy and would then masturbate supposedly for our entertainment, and we, that's me and my sisters, kept his dirty little secret. I just gave thanks that he never asked us to participate. His tenure was brief as after a few months he got a job close to his home in the country. I wondered if they realised what he had been doing to small children and if other children would have to put up with it. How do parents and friends miss what is happening? Why do they leave it to the child to report the perpetrators? I do want to warn someone indeed anyone who even just suspects something and does nothing that you are just as responsible as the fiend who messes with that little child. How cruel!

I have to say and quite forcibly that because of her **cringe** activities none of us would ever confide in our mother. That's so sad and so cruel. Why didn't she notice?

Please don't stand back and do nothing. You are the one who can to stop the monsters and end the horrors facing someone you love or someone you know but it takes courage to take notice, accept responsibility and ask questions. All it takes is just speaking out but carefully. They may thank you for all of their lives. I believe that means you may also save a life or two.

When I started to write this story I was focusing on what abuse did to me. The real effect of abuse of the child can radiate out in the future and affect a partner, a marriage and in many cases, a whole unsuspecting family.

And the real effect is related to how we handle trust and who we are likely to reject because they remind us of someone who turned us into a 'trollop'. Don't ever sound like you are judging the person. The reason that they haven't told anybody will be that they are too scared. Affected children are destined to become furious.

Thankfully these days professionals like teachers and GPs are trained to pick up the clues and sometimes they do but sadly, they are often not so sure.

The need to be speaking out is urgent. Keeping quiet is something is suspected in nothing short of criminal.

Even if they speak out as they should, friends and family members on the frontline may prefer to ignore or even deny something not so nice. It is only so very recently that after the good work of the Australian of the Year Grace Tame that child victims were allowed to speak out about the abuse and the perpetrator after the law was changed.

Don't let the truth go unnoticed. The monsters lie low until the next opportunity. It can go on in the shadows. Bad news! Trust yourself! If you only think that maybe you saw something you probably did. Let me tell you that a person is most certainly also complicit when they just look away. Don't look away. Seek the help of experts.

I am real. Maudie does exist. My story is real. This is what I discovered when I started out to try and make sense of what happened when I was very young. I can look now at how the failure of more than one marriage affected my life and that of another. I use my story to honour my father who lost his kids all because his spouse was infected by a severe bout of **furiousity** cleverly crafted to his own sick advantage by a dashing part-time paedophile. Mr. Smelly Perp in this story invaded the world of two small children belonging to a fractured family feeding on the sadness, misery, hatred, blame and hurt of a world that had not been left behind. He didn't work alone. He had help from a string of stupid and furious relatives.

The reason for using the word 'furious' here is because I believe that the person who suspects or even hears that there is a 'perpetrator in the house' is both angry at the victim and the perp because it is a 'bloody inconvenience' and an embarrassment . That's why **furiousity** kicks in.

I can say quite definitely that the real culprit in this lack of sharing and asking for help was the lack of trust that I had in my mother because all she ever did was treat me with disrespect and make me feel so ashamed and useless.

There was the family curse I know now did exist and of course it was **furiousity**. The curse was nothing but a decision made about an event was another matter altogether. I found someone to trust and that kept me sane. Because he didn't hear me the problem kept appearing every 4th Sunday. Something in me is thankful that he didn't hear as I now know he would have taken to Uncle Jerk with his bare hands. But the point is that I had an avenue through which I could express my pain and it made me stronger. My mother had been successful in establishing an impenetrable wall because she insisted on her verbal abuse she thought she had a right to use as she wanted.

Nobody queried it. Not one person seems to have stopped to ask why.

Nobody fought for justice. Nobody looked for a way out. Nobody made a stand for anything at all. Nobody said, "Let's not pass this on to our family and our unsuspecting descendants". I think that's because those on her side of the family were so used to **cringe** that they thought it was perfectly normal.

Obviously nobody had ever said, 'Let's not pass this on to Lillian". Well they did and Lillian who always thought she was the clever one in all her dealings with family and friends, is the one that died alone.

My story didn't start out redacted but by the time I had finished, I knew I had to hide the identity of many of the people involved, regardless of whether I was accusing them of anything or not. Here each real name might be changed and sometimes it's not. It really doesn't matter because most of them are dead anyway. I don't hear so much of the **furiousity** today because the ones who were so very sure that they were entitled to 'tell it like it is' are long dead. As soon as I was close to finishing my story, I shared what I was writing about with others who are still living. I should have known how they could react. I should have expected to be told by both friends and family that I should keep silent because they found the whole subject just a little too 'twee'. They were the ones still doing it. Sometimes they weren't the ones I expected would be against me writing this and speaking out. I felt abused all over again. I was again being told to be silent by someone who started from the premise that it never happened. It was just like the story of being molested.

It was so like before. What had changed?

That was devastating for me because I was back there with a secret nobody wanted me to tell. I was sure that the only one who wanted to listen was George. It hurt. I was back where I had been so many years before with all the same old feelings of shame, guilt, separation, regret, rejection and doubt. All I had wanted to do is tell the truth and now I was faced with shame. It was shame, shame and more shame.

"You Poor Thing"

Now I knew why I never told another soul while the molestation of my body and soul was in progress. I was so used to the kind of abuse and blaming that went on in most other things. If I told my mother or grandmother about some sort of success I had I would be accused of skiting and drawing attention to myself.

My achievements were always hidden and even made shameful. I knew that telling the story of Uncle Jerk could have led to the sympathy vote but it would not be long before the fury started. I was mortified when I found out for myself what a trollop and a tart meant as a description of what girls and women do that's bad. I was sure I was now guilty of some pretty terrible stuff. I would ask some of my friends only to find myself in front of a teacher and accused of talking dirty. I have no idea if any adult ever spoke to my mother. I doubt it. She would have been angrier.

The sympathy can often sound like understanding but it ends up like

"Please don't tell me any more sordid details."

"That stuff should all remain hidden. What about the man's family and our family for that matter? You are so very thoughtless."

"Wouldn't it be better just to let sleeping dogs lie?"

"How do we know whether you brought it on yourself?"

"You need to get your facts right before you say anything and that's for everybody's sake."

"Isn't it better to just let it all go? It's in the past".

Each of these comments made me want to confront all the parents and tell everyone to protect their children. I would then probably be accused of trying to shame all the grandpas and uncles in town. I'm not out to get anyone. I am not after compensation or retribution. But I do want to show how hard it is to face the truth and apportion blame when what you are fighting is ignorance and **furiousity**. And it doesn't stop a perp.

I really want to show the reader how to apportion responsibility. I do want a state of alert to stop it happening to any small child. I just want to save a life or two. If only I could. If only I could. There is something quite profound and clear in all of this. No child is ever guilty of abuse of an adult. We are the children not the ones at fault.

Why do they call us 'Little tarts'? My mother used to make jam tarts and lemon tarts. I loved them. What do they mean when they called children 'tarts'? I heard a woman call her child a 'tart' one day in a supermarket when the little girl was pestering for sweets. It sent a shiver down my back. I found myself looking again at the child and there was the wince I had seen so many times before. I wanted to scream at the woman and tell her to stop. Of course I didn't do that. I should have said, "Jam tarts, Yummee." I chickened out.

I used to write poems about my trauma and this is one I remember well

> I've got a secret I can't tell
> I have to keep the secret very well
> It isn't very nice. It isn't very good
> Why did I promise that I would?
> I want to scream. I want to cry. Oh how I wish that
> man would die.
> Die you, you dirty fiend!
> He's dead of course.
> Oh yes! The secret is mine forever and I just don't
> want to have to keep owning it.
> Am I still a little tart Mum?

In my world 'Perp' is just something I used for myself when I was much older to describe the nasty, smelly person I had to face and in my face once a month. I remember only that someone told me that their uncle looked like a 'Perp'. I was to later find out it was a short form of 'Perpetrator'. But I didn't know what that meant until I was approaching my teen years. I thought everybody had 'perps' in their lives and it mean you had to find ways to stay away from them. Now I think of it like the word 'penetrator' because they get into your soul, your heart and your mind regardless of what they might do to your body. Sometimes Perps hide in plain sight. Sometimes they are in the shadows. When they enter your world, the prospect of yet another one entering and taking over your life is always there.

Oh Boy! Did I have one of those? Yes, I did! I had my own all singing all dancing Perp and years later I was, for some time, quite sure I had killed him. I decided I must have killed him with magic or a childish version of voodoo calling up a silly curse my mother said was rife and very dangerous in our family. I even made up my own mumbo jumbo.

That wasn't long before I had realised that there was something silly about my mother and before I realised that I didn't have to take the blame for everything she said about me being bad when I was just very sad and miserable. Is it possible that my mother was mean because she was just plain silly?

I was a teenager before I started to see my mother as a silly person. I didn't ever understand her flakiness and the way she apportioned all of the blame for our unhappiness sideways onto to my dear deaf dad. And then there was the madness of always blaming a stupid curse for everything while I was sure the only one to blame was Lillian. She was the one who couldn't be trusted.

Until the point when I wondered what my silly mother had been up to I was so sure that the family fights and our unhappiness was possibly my fault and that I was a very bad person. As I grew older I became convinced that it was not my fault that I fought to discard the attentions of the Perp to the extent that someone else's life was ruined and that someone else turned out to be a monster. In my mind that meant that I must have tried to kill her too. I must have killed off everything nice about her. She was my sister.

Kiddee fiddling is a nasty topic that many people would prefer not to know anything about. Some people think that children can't help but put out signals that they want to be fondled and fiddled with. If only I could save someone from turning into some sort of a victim as they grew up. Or stop them becoming the black sheep of the family thinking they were very bad and wrong worried and guilty for all of their lives.

Sometimes we are manipulated into silence with praise we don't get from those we love. In my case it was all about princesses and crowns and special qualities I had. It was all 'piffle'.

And I just want the world to know that despite the numerous media reports, enquiries and royal commissions into children and abuse associated with churches, care institutions and educational organisations, abuse can be in the home, a neighbourhood or conducted by individuals anywhere and the victim will have been specifically chosen. Of course they are chosen because they don't have the skills to protect themselves and will certainly not know what to say to alert others to their plight.

But wait, there will be signs. I am talking to you who are also the gatekeepers. You, the parents, grandparents and families in general have to stay on guard as the Perps are still at it somewhere out there in kiddee-land and maybe it's very close to home and right under your busy elsewhere noses.

Or it is a subject you would rather not know about or face? It was a very young and innocent little me that the Perp focused on. I don't intend to get your attention by telling you lurid tales of what he did to me. Some of it you will already be able to guess. What I want to tell you is that it happened continuously because my mother was a **cringe** expert and I didn't trust her enough to tell her and I didn't really think I could do anything to change her.

I do remember that I felt so very helpless. A few years later I would have had a sad face. Or maybe it was there already. I want to tell you why I was a helpless target of a kiddee fiddler and how each Perp is likely to be able to set the scene unhindered, keep up some sort of interpersonal relationship with gatekeepers, only do things that don't leave any marks and manage to convince their prey that he or she is to blame and must keep the secret.

This target always thought she was to blame for things that hurt her. He managed to convince me that I would make my Mum and Dad happy only if I did what he wanted and only if I let him do what he wanted to me. Of course I knew nothing at all about what was right or wrong. He managed to convince me that if I told anyone about what we did together I would miss out on everything including birthdays, Christmas and even Easter eggs. And of course my parents would stop loving me. I didn't want my mother to be more furious with me so I kept quiet about everything.

It's only now that I am old and hiding the grey hairs that I can tell you a story about me, my sister, my Mum and Dad and my sometimes strange family with a history that had my mother diving for the Ouija board and going to fortune tellers. I would give anything to go back and warn everyone about the danger that wasn't a stranger but in my case I would have had to warn them about their own ignorance and neglect because I was just a kid after all.

I waited until just before they died to tell each of them. My mother called me a liar and my dad cried in my arms. Why couldn't I rely on those around me who should have noticed my hurt and my pain? I have spent so much of my life trying not to be angry and always being confused about where blame must lie. Now I know that if my Dad was here he would be telling me it isn't here with me. Being able to share with him meant that I didn't live my life in shame. I picked myself up, dusted myself off and kept going safe in the knowledge that my Dad loved me.

And by the way, I am here to tell you that victim blaming is another form of **furiousity**. And always acting up and getting into trouble is also a form of **furiousity**. And I know after all, even when I had turned six or seven, I was much too young to know what I could have done to outsmart him and expose him without having to pass him on to my younger sister. I would look for ways to be naughty hoping to be punished by not being allowed t go out to the chook house or go for a walk with that man in the forest. What was my alternative? I thought I had to do that but she didn't deserve it and if only I had known how much her life would be affected by that knob-wobbler who was addicted to messing with little children, their bodies and their minds. I tried it seemed forever to say sorry to my sister but it fell on deaf ears.

Was it my fault? I wanted someone to notice but they just let me down. I took the blame and now I know why. Little children should expect to be happy and safe. Our family would have appeared to most observers to be quite normal. In all the photos there we were most presentable, well dressed and you could have described my Mum and Dad as a 'very nice young couple with nice kids'.

We looked very happy and safe when we were photographed as a family.

I thought we were just like everyone else but when I would bravely whisper in some little friend's ear and ask them about their Perps they would run screaming to grownups and I would be threatened with having my mouth washed out with soap. I knew not to do that as often it probably meant being sent to Coventry. Most of the time I felt everybody had let me down but I wasn't really sure I was entitled to feel that way. George had never said anything about my behaviour or that it was my fault.

I was so frightened of the man who molested me and of anyone who looked like him or smelt like him. That fear of uncles, other people's dads and milkmen stayed with me all of my life even though my Perp was and remains dead and hopefully buried deep or burned in Hell. He had made me at times mistrust my dad. He made me mistrust any men who would reach out for a hug and a kiss like they would with other children. The only exception to the rule was my step-grandfather who I believed would never hurt a fly. Pop lived in another state and I know I would have told him about Jerk if he had been here more often. George grew up with Pop in his life and I am sure that it was his stepfather's common sense that helped Him deal with his disability.

I trusted my step-grandfather as much as I trusted my dad. I could see where Dad got his gentleness from. Pop never had a bad word to say about his stepson. Because he visited us only at Christmas I never got the chance to share with him. But I thought I had shared with my Dad.

I do remember that one auntie (a family friend) had said that there was something quite weird about me. At that time in my life I didn't know what she meant and I hated our visits to their house. I do now realize that the weirdness she saw in me was her concern about me leaving their male dominated house and wandering alone for hours along the rows of flowers and vegetables in their huge market garden. I would be chastised again but that was small punishment while the risk seemed to be always there that one of the males would choose to take me away from everyone. This story is not just about the Perp. I would not give him that satisfaction.

I really did worry a lot about who I was with and whether they would do anything to hurt me.

I have realised for such a long time that before I leave this world I need to tell all the parents and grandparents who are not paying attention and who let stuff happen to the small humans they are or were supposed to be looking after, that it was and will always be their fault. I have to pass on that news in the only way I know how.

There is no way that an abused child will look and act completely normal. The biggest giveaway is a child that looks guilty and somewhat defiant.

Another giveaway would have been described by my sisters as being 'weird'.

I did have some strange thoughts. The Perp who couldn't keep his hands to himself deserved to have his weenie wound round the nearest lamp post and hit by a bus. (I love that scenario).

That Perp was clever by half. He must have thought he had successfully turned my mother into a love struck schoolgirl and idiot devotee and my father into a floundering fool watching his silly wife just to make sure that the Perp wasn't into her knickers.

I wanted the Perp to die and I finally got my wish. What a crazy mix of horror, guilt and pleasure that greeted this nine-year-old every day of her life? He deserved his punishment but why did I have to go on wondering for much of my life whether it was my fault. "Why don't you hear me? Why don't you notice? I know I should have stopped thinking that the fault was with me? It was always with me wasn't it? My silly mother Lillian should have known what was happening. It was Sunday.

It was time for cold meat and salad and wine trifle without the wine. It seemed that I was the only tasty bit on offer.

Why didn't she know? They can all see me can't they? They can see how he takes me away from them. Why don't they stop it? They watch me go and they smile. They must know how I feel. I want to be sick. Surely they see. Lillian must have seen how attentive Uncle Jerk was. Was she that naïve?

How I wish I could have turned to my parents and say, "I need you to stop him George. I need you to send him away Lillian. Please stop him now. One of you should be standing up for me. Don't you know what he does? Don't make me go with the monster. Please notice. The monster has me under his control."

If I had my time over again I would know now that I could have painted Jerk's old fellow with a navy blue texta colour. Then I could leave the questions to Auntie Jerk. Foresight is not the realm of the young. If only we could think strategically. We would be in control.

"It Isn't Here"

Gentle George was my lovely father. Lately I have found myself chatting to him though not through the power of my mobile phone or on social media but in my imagination. I think he hovers and would talk back to me if I knew how to make contact with the dead. I think about him when I can't sleep and at that empty time in a long sleepless night when I fancy I can hear his voice and I know he would whisper to me, "It isn't here".

We used to have a running joke that I would lose my sense of humour and he would play word games trying to find it for me. When I come to think of it, his lip reading skills were incredible. Sometimes it would be the question of where I had dropped my bottom lip. He would place notes around the garden that said "it isn't here".

George still helps me find things. I know that sounds silly but that's really his job now that he is in heaven. If I lose my keys or my car in a car park I turn to George and eventually that which was lost turns up. Of course George could do nothing to help with all those years that I thought I was so soiled that I should hide myself away but he had, without knowing why, told me that I was stronger than I thought and that I could beat the lot of them.

Of course I realise that it is the lessons that Dad taught me that have stayed with me all this time and I want to remember them always. Dad breathed his last in his early seventies. His death and his subsequent absence from the scene would have made it even easier for some of my mother's family and my silly sisters to continue to claim he was the bad parent and grief giver. It was Dad who, had they had known about me and my sister, would get the blame from some in Mum's family for any misery and grief in our family. The tendency to blame the one who was already to blame for something else was another stupid reason why I didn't tell them.

I didn't know why all blame was his to bear. I was sure that that they would never blame my mother if I had told them what had happened. That's **furiousity** for you. My mother, Lillian, entered the pearly gates at the beginning of this story would blame Dad for her misery until she left us. She would still be claiming it was his fault because he didn't want to listen and didn't want to dance. She was mean and cruel about anything at all to do with George who loved her till the day he died.

I should call my Mum 'Spinning Lillian' in recognition of the amount of spin she put on her stories of my Dad's guilt about almost everything. She would have been happy with that moniker for another much crazier reason. She really thought she had been forced by fate to be an unhappy wife and mother instead of a flashy ballroom dancer and notable dressmaker. She wasn't too flashy of course but she blamed that on poor deaf husband who could never dance a step to save himself.

The man who couldn't dance was right when he said "You have what you need". I was too young to understand that he was right. I was really too young to understand what he meant but I felt sure he was on my side. After all, I had been able to share everything with him, or so I thought.

When I was a lot older and I had rationalised that my mother was in love with her dance partner or the Pride of Erin and for a short while I thought that perhaps she was jealous of me.

I tried to figure out what made Lillian tick. I saw an exotic film script or maybe it was the subject of a nineteenth century novelette that could have ended with my heroic dad shooting his rival at one hundred paces and just to make it even more ironic in the right foot so that the dancing was finished and done with. Jerk died of a heart attack so I didn't need to do any dreaming. This is getting quite bizarre. Let's get down to tin tacks. I was abused as a very small child and it was not by either of my parents. This is not a book with all the gruesome details although I do mention knobs and dangly bits at times. Much of what happened to me is hidden deep and festers inside my personal and private memory bank. But it was long ago.

I was the one who was being trained to hide it because they made it very clear that I had no right to speak out. I choose to keep it hidden and avoid blurting my story out when I hear similar stories or when I have met some kind, friendly and caring soul. The ***cringe*** took care of my need to reach out to the person who seemed to care the least. I mention this because the practice does serve to alienate the listener. I did desperately want my mother to love me but she kept proving to me that it was furthest from her mind and I didn't know how to change that.

As a victim I knew I would have had to protect myself from the doubters, the "**don't worry dear, it will go away**" lot or those who just can't believe it at all.

Then, there are those who tell me I should have been psychologically assessed by a kid psychologist or someone into hymen inspections. They talk about false memories.

I don't think Lillian ever realised how much I was traumatised by her words like,

"Isn't that jumper a bit too tight?" *or*
"If I had my way, I'd rub all that tacky stuff off your face".

Why did she have to say those things? She said it for no reason that I could see. Was that one of the moments when she remembered that Jerk didn't seem to want her? Were the attacks on me so automatic that she wasn't really aware she was saying them? Did she know how they landed?

Very often blame would be shifted from me to my Dad when it became convenient and I didn't want that to happen either. I look back now and if Lillian was here right now I would say "How dare you make a small child take the blame for something which through ignorance or malice you chose to ignore and even encourage. It was your fault if you weren't watching, you suspected something or you knew and I was too young to understand what was happening."

Before worried Mums and Dads jump to impossible conclusions, I am not asking parents to go overboard in protecting their children from every lovely old Grandpa who just wants a cuddle. I am not asking you to run over the young man who just retrieved your son's cricket ball or the dad of a classmate who helped your precious little girl put on her overcoat. I am certainly not condoning you going overboard in the search for neighbourhood paedophiles. It's not about knowing who the Perps are. It's about being vigilant. It's about trusting the kids. This is only ever about knowing your children and knowing when and why they are sad, unhappy and worried about something.

A sad, unhappy and worried child doesn't start out that way. A naughty, bad tempered child might just be angry or just might be in danger. The anger may be all to do with you. If it's not, check it out.

And if you are a proponent of 'good old family **cringe**' nobody will confide in you. And anger is catching. Without Dad I would have caught anger from Lillian who seemed to instinctively know what to say to make you feel dreadful.

And here is something you might not know. If you are angry all of your life you will never be ready to see straight. You will not be able to see when somebody is winding you up because fury is their only game. You won't know to make sure that your children or even one child doesn't get to pass your fury on. I didn't learn that from observing my mother and her need to make a passionate defence of her anger, distress, meanness, ability to discriminate, refusal to support, readiness to scorn and her tendency to show a lack of appreciation and to focus on brutality as a God given right. I learned it was something she made up from a Dad who loved her more than she ever deserved. I learned that from his readiness to forgive and forget.

Here I sit at the arse end of my life wondering if things all through my life could have been different. Would I be so different or indifferent if I hadn't just been me with all my ignorance and failings and who had a mother who didn't seem to care?

What if those responsible for delivering all the inspiring, positive and reliable lessons that life had to offer along the way had been up to scratch? Do I have to continue to sheet home the blame at my own feet or even on my own shoulders? Should I be forever chastising myself sure that had I ever listened to the right people I might have avoided trying to find a place to hide away from trauma? Does the blame lie somewhere else? I hear the ghost of my father. He is saying loud and clearly,

"It's not here, My Dear".

It can't be news to those in charge such as parents and grandparents that children are not born angry, fearful, wary, badly behaved, belligerent, deceitful, sad, aggressive, whining and simply awful to live with. Something is very wrong and if you don't ask yourself why you don't deserve to have them in the first place.

And is it at all possible that you have unwittingly used **cringe** and left that child unsure of who they were and who they could trust? Is it at all possible that your **cringe** set up a difficult and unworkable relationship with that child? How can you forget the importance of trust?

If, as a parent, you are into **cringe**, and your child has no alternative other than to not trust you, is that the price you really want to pay? Surely not!

Because of my mother's need to get stuck into me and keep me at a distance I had to accept that everything that was being done to me was my fault. Blaming children for what an adult does to them is the cruelest thing I can think of. Being angry with the child because someone molests or hurts them is callous. Letting children take the blame is grotesque.

And have I got news for someone like my Mum. If being furious is all you know to do and what to feel you will always look for the fury in everything that comes your way, you will never know how to forgive. You will never see another way out. You will always want to hurt people as much as you can and you will be a real shit to be with. When you are dying your daughter will pack her bags and head for a place as far away as possible. You will die alone. You will deserve just that.

Perps hide in the shadows and the malignant side of their character maybe hiding behind someone very likeable and popular. I don't know anything about my Perp. Apparently he was a good dancer not like some movie star but perfect with Lillian who thought she could have been partner to one of the film stars. I didn't want to share a secret with that man. George was film star handsome but Jerk looked like a bad ad for hair gel. I have no knowledge of his dancing skills but they must have been pretty good for my mother to stake her marriage on her once a week dancing and once a month cold dinners. But I do remember that men were scarce because of the war. Dancing partners must have been even harder to find.

Having a sordid secret makes their victim two-faced as well. I know and I always have known that something, in this case someone bad, had made me different to everybody else. I never saw any evidence that other people had to put up with the same thing but of course it could well have been their story and they fearfully hid it. I didn't know why I messed up but everything was in my mind pointing to a failing on my watch. I saw it with penitent eyes.

Why did I have to do that? Maybe I could reasonably decide it had to be my fault after all and I was sure that I should have handled it much better. I remember telling myself that it just wasn't fair. I kept looking for clues as to what to do and how to behave. I didn't realise that it could never have been my fault and that somebody was doing something very, very bad to me and it seemed it was with everybody else's agreement. I don't believe for one minute that Jerk ever bedded my mother. I will never know if I am right or wrong but I have heard that men who fancy children like to leave the women alone. Maybe that made her even more angry.

And I also had George so I didn't really miss her love and affection. You can't have love and affection without trust anyway so it was reciprocal.

All That Blame

"I HEAR YOU DAD. I DON'T BLAME YOU. I PROMISE." THAT WAS WHAT I shared with the ghost of my dear dead dad for as long as I can remember. When George died when he was over seventy I was still trying to work out who needed forgiveness. I have long given up trying to blame someone else.

It wasn't a person that did their worst it was an idea. The idea was that **furiousity** must be worn like a badge and preserved through the generations. It has to stop now and I think I know how to do it. Stand fast. Stand solid. Stand true. Stand generous. Stand loyal. Stand firm. Stand for being a serious interruption but only to **furiousity cringe**.

While the Perp was busy wrecking my life, and later that of my sister, mother Lillian was very busy turning our family into a painful, yelling, screaming and hateful mess. She would scream at Dad who didn't hear her. That would make her scream even more and then she would scream at us but we would be switched off. Everyone would scream at my little brother. To my sisters that would seem as though it was George's fault because they thought he wouldn't listen. That was what she claimed. They were too young to understand about his lip reading skills.

Could I have been stronger and louder and better at standing up for myself? Could I have been better at standing up for dear deaf George? Could I have enlisted the help of other people in the family? Why did nobody in the family see that there was anything wrong?

Should I have known what to do to keep myself safe? Would I have been able to fight for myself and be more loved?

Why didn't I have the right words?

Why was it that I was always fighting to hide the tears and

sadness while I seemed to have been surrounded by happy, smiley faces always pushing me towards the person I feared so much? All of that suggested to me that I was in the wrong. Somehow I deserved what was being done to me. Where was the proof that I was OK? Was I ever going to be in charge of what happened to me? Was I cursed? Was I the only one who was abused among my friends and school mates or was it happening all around me and to people who hid their own pain and sadness behind their hands?

Why didn't I trust my Dad enough to tell him what was happening in a place where he couldn't protect me? He seemed to have enough on his plate.

Was I just a bit unlucky after all? This, and all the other questions, hundreds of them stayed with me at school, at work and at play even though some of the detail of the assault has remained hidden deep in my memory and probably always will. It was to only bubble to the surface when I later heard the stories of others. But the pain of helplessness and worthlessness had always stayed with me and affected my life as a child and as a young woman who spent all of her time trying to avoid falling into a trap that looked anything like the horrors of the past. Instead of celebrating my achievements and successes as I grew older I just congratulated myself for staying alive and staying angry with that horrible man.

I knew I would be OK if I stayed well out of reach of perverts. This meant staying away from everything or everyone that posed any kind of threat or anyone who would find out about my failings. My mother's reliance on **cringe** showed me I could never reach out to her. Why is it that we want our children to act like they are growing up and yet we just might be leaving them with no skills whatsoever? My sisters learned the **furiousity** regime from my mother. They didn't really know George because they believed her stories. Lillian's influence and her stories were designed to poison their relationship with their father.

I don't need to ask my surviving sister whether she always said things that belittled them and discriminated against George as she had done all of my life it seems. Our mother was intent on keeping us as enemies.

Lillian would deliver messages like

"You're a great sister aren't you?
Did you get a kick out of thumbing your nose at the people
who worry where your next meal is coming from?
You don't care about any of us."

I thought that was bad but **cringe** was worse. I can tell you how much I dearly wanted to find a life partner who would not only understand my sadness and fear but love me enough to wipe clean the dirt and trauma of the past. How could I have known that one day I would find that person lacking and incapable of loving me like that? It was devastating not only because I couldn't use our relationship to heal but because as a tiny boy, still grieving for his dead mother, he was dragged into the hideous games of foul men who used him for their pleasure?

They left him to try to create a life that was honourable and fulfilling but they had killed off all hope. The worst part was that it was the hope that he could open his arms wide even to someone like me. Even to someone who wanted to love him. He went on to reject that love all of his life. I just didn't know his pain.

Very recently I listened to a TV documentary where a retired priest confessed to molesting boys and claiming that God had most certainly forgiven him for his transgressions. Liar! Liar! Liar! He lied to them and he lies to all of us.

What about the saying that goes something like, "Whosever

harms one of God's little ones does harm to God himself"? He was using the wages of sin to claim a victory with God's forgiveness. I don't know about his God but my God does not support the right of paedophiles to ruin lives. Any God in my mind abhors the kiddee fiddler and knows how I wanted to rush to his side with a sharp knife and with a male abuser, cut his ugly knob off.

He was doing much to destroy faith in a God that was loving and just. From a young age I had lost my trust in a God who I thought had left me to struggle with the guilt only to find out that it was never mine to own anyway.

It might not surprise you that by that stage I had decided that God didn't love me at all because I didn't know how to stop what was happening to me. I had deduced that I must be too young to ask God for help. Later, I didn't know how to wipe the slate clean. I didn't know that I was lovable at all and that I was always entitled to protect my own safety. I didn't know if my parents weren't aware of what was happening. And maybe God was furious with me as well. I often thought that my love for my Dad was behind the whole thing. I would often watch other people with their parents and notice that mothers had a tendency to hug and praise. What on earth was wrong with Lillian that she could never reach out to soothe, support or praise? Why was there nobody on Lillian's side of the family who seemed to know anything of unconditional love?

I didn't know that the blame wasn't with Dad just as it wasn't with me. It is not only the choirboys and altar boys who have suffered from attacks by these creatures, the paedos who will ask where was God in all of this? It is all the people that the victims have loved and who loved them and then we go on to wonder why they even went so far as to take their own lives because God hadn't listened.

It is the disciplinarians who wonder why that child is so out of control and screwed up. Why is it that nobody notices their pain and asks why they are not like other children? It is not only us little girls in our frilly dresses and colourful bows in our hair that are hurt by these monsters. It's any child of either sex who can find themselves under the control of some hideous adult with an evil mind willing to virtually kill off innocence and ruin the childhood of the vulnerable for their own grotesque pleasure.

A Very Serious Interruption

It's time to stop making it easy for them. It's time to train parents in what is a huge and complex area of child psychology that this much is simple. Pay attention! Pay attention! Pay attention! Train parents to know all they can of risk management and what is expected of them in protecting the rights of the child to be safe, loved and childlike. The alternative is not pretty. But the solution isn't rocket science. It needs to be talked about.

It begins with a simple greeting like,

"And here's my wonderful daughter".

Can you imagine what it is like to be watching the faces of your parents who don't see that you are being forced to sit in the lap of your Perp who has a hard-on? I just wanted someone to ask why I was looking so angry or sad. Yes! There in the lounge room of the Perp's home.

I couldn't see his face but he had won once again. This was all like a grotesque pantomime. Every child that is ever sexually abused is different to every other.

Every abuser is different but that is still no excuse for families failing to see what is happening and failing to know how to help each child to live a safe, confident and happy life. That was one of those awful times when you wished the Perp's house would burn down and you could be saved by a serious interruption. My story was about what happened in my parent's bad marriage as all parents should know that a happy marriage can also be fertile ground for confusion.

In my particular case it was the constant focus on **cringe** that would establish a dangerous place where the ghosts of the Perps hang out.

Perps thrive in **cringe** environments. They feed on the insecurity and rejection.

I know in the long term I was so very lucky because even through the prism of his unhappiness and grief, my dad was able to give me some important tools that I could go on to use in such a way as to give my life meaning. More than anything else he let me share. I was never going to share with an antagonist.

I didn't know it at the time but he had unwittingly given me what I needed to use my anger wisely and rise above the sadness and the pain. But I look back and know that I lived some of my childhood in a kind of stupor. Maybe I would find someone someday who would protect me and not want to abuse me and make me unhappy. I kept looking for a man I could trust and a person I could share my story with. I wasn't furious. I was just so very sad.

I didn't get to reach out to hold and comfort the man I married because I couldn't see that he was just like me. I didn't know the things that had happened to him until it was clear that we couldn't be together. It was well into our time apart that I learned from his older brother that my spouse had been abused as a small child. My never-was a real partner was even younger than me while those who should have cared might as well have just stood and watched. They were just guilty of gross ignorance. This was about people who lived a religious life and for their own weird reasons chose not to notice or care. Of course he didn't know what that meant to me because he didn't know how I was hurting for the same reason. And I found out about his screwed up life after our marriage was over. I didn't see the hurt in his eyes or if I did, I thought I had caused it. Had I been able to share my story perhaps I could have helped him in some way.

Probably not! Maybe it was too late. Of course it was. By the time I found out it was too late to raise the subject without hurting him.

Is there any way that the serious interruptions my father had used would have worked? I didn't try because I didn't see that his **furiousity** was just as strong as my mother's. I remember that Dad would have said to a furious, yelling, red in the face Lillian,

"***Hold on Phyllis, I have to get the phone***".

While not the exact words because we didn't have a phone, this would be one of George's serious interruptions.

Lillian would be forced to acknowledge that the man she had been verbally abusing had just left the room. George would have managed to do that without being nasty or cruel. I always knew he was being kind.

When I was seventeen, my father disappeared from my life. Jerk was dead and I thought I was free of the confusion, sadness, guilt and shame. It doesn't work like that. Dad re-appeared many years later when my brother was dying. That's when I remembered all of his anti-**cringe** activities.

We had never had a conversation about the origin of his word games when I was growing up. I had heard stories of how his mother was forced by general attitudes of others, particularly employers and as a single mum had decided to place a very young George in a children's home on the border of New South Wales and Victoria. Of course he ran away and walked back to Melbourne looking for her.

I never found out where he learned to say things that would leave him feeling stronger. When you suffer from **furiousity** you are diminished. You have lost big time and the things that they say about you are going to stay there in your memory. If you are a serious interruption anything can happen. If people accused George of being deaf he would say "***Yes of course my dear. All three ears.***"

When asked what that meant he would tell them that he used to have another ear and it fell off. Sometimes he would tell them that the third one was his 'rear'.

Looking back at what Lynette taught me I can assure you it was a simple as turning on the bully and telling them they are so handsome or pretty if it was coming from the girls. Lynette would focus on the right ear and say something like "***Oops. Something just flew out of your ear***". Another tactic was to ask the bully if they sing and if they know 'Danny Boy'.

I learnt to ask my Nasty Nana if she ever got to speak to the Queen. It was a reminder of a poem I wrote for her. The poem was a reference to her dream of being presented to royalty. When you live on a share farm on the top of a mountain range and only have the kids and the chickens to converse with it's easy to imagine that one day you will be invited to afternoon with the Royal Family Windsor.

Then, and only then, might you ever consent to be photographed with a young Prince or Princess. You might extend that to the child of a lady in waiting or the Prime Minister. This had all come about because there had been some weird story that an ancestor on my great grandmother's side was descendant of Mary Queen of Scots. There is nothing in historical records to show that to be true.

I wrote many poems dedicated to someone's strange belief that we were probably ascended from royalty and would find out sooner or later that they wanted to meet us. I used questions associated with the poem to ward of my Nasty Nana's **cringe** and it worked so much that she would sometimes greet me with an answer. It was working. She would say something like

"Don't worry the sign is back on the front door."

This poem was my triumph and after a while I realised she really prefer our game to the tirade of abuse I has been used to. I think that's where I got a taste for writing silly poems. It worked with my grandmother but Lillian wasn't interested.

We just had a call from the royal aide
Who told us the Queen was here.
The wind blew the sign off our front door
That said "Please go round to the rear"
My mother just sat and cried and cried
So much she couldn't speak
But, the telephone rang with the nicest news
She'll be back on Sunday week. Rule Britannia.

Because of the way that Nasty Nana was and the way that she had always greeted me with her **cringe** talk, I imagined that the Queen and members of the royal household were always into inferior speak. Did they always tell a visitor to 'stand up straight and look presentable'? That's the approach that Lillian took and of course she was unaware that the 'Princess' image was the one that Jerk had used to ingratiate himself. I used to feel like screaming when Lillian went 'all royal on us'.

Though I would get it off my chest by writing other silly poems I was always too scared to show them to her. But it did come in handy when I was putting together my list of retorts.

I can remember a particular occasion when I was getting the rounds of the kitchen from a furious mother when I felt the need to throw my schoolbag down the hall and scream loudly that it was the princess I saw at the station.

Mum thought I had a fit but when I walked back in she had forgotten all about her gripe that had nothing at all to do with me.

Her opening remark to me had been,

***Well little princess. If someone was to visit I couldn't show them your room because your bed is not made and the staff are all dead from hard work*".**

That morning I had been running late because I had been helping Lillian put the washing out before she went off to work. I was very ashamed because I had been made an example by the headmistress in front of the whole school. I was waiting to use some spectacular response to the outburst that was to come so that I could make the right kind of serious but powerful interruption I had learned from George. I knew not to put her down or make her feel insignificant. It is also most important to note that I was the only one of her children that stayed with her to the end. Or maybe it was almost the end. By the way, Lillian did get to meet the Queen's sister when much later in her life she worked as a waitress for a caterer to the rich and famous.

I didn't trust my mother. She had spent some time with the head mistress and I felt sure she was putting me down. I was never going to know. If she would say all those bad things to me why wouldn't she say them to someone at the school. After that occasion I couldn't settle and I was so very determined to give up school and it wasn't too long before I did. It had never quite sunk in for me that I was turning down a virtual scholarship to one of the best schools in the State. My mother was never interested in education for her children and she was never going to stop me from leaving.

Sometimes I would hear that my mother had been singing my praises behind my back. None of that made any sense at all because she still did the **cringe** routine to put me back in my place it seems. When I did finally love someone enough to take a risk on all the mushy stuff it was the friend of my very dearest friends.

The company I was keeping included my very best friend,

the delightful Faithfull Flo. F-Flo came into my life on the return journey from one Church Easter camp when she entered the carriage where I sat alone and plopping down beside me like a beached whale announced that I had stolen her boyfriend. Said boyfriend had been lurking outside the carriage like a silly schoolboy and I realised that he had joined me on one of our late night hikes when we were known to march two by two through the town through places like cemeteries and town parks.

This was all news to me. My answer was to write his name on a piece of paper and hand it back to her. I had laryngitis for much of the time we were there and he thought it was funny to tease me and try to translate for me. F-Flo had watched on helplessly and while neither of us wanted to pursue the relationship with 'mister might have been wonderful', me and my new friend, the girls he had managed to lose became the closest of close friends and I wouldn't have hurt her for a start. We both watched on as he became betrothed to another from the same church.

Over the years that followed my friendship with Flo became stronger and when she married the man of her dreams I was her bridesmaid. My dear friend and her man introduced me to a group of friends I could trust and I knew it was time to look for someone to share my life with. I was looking for someone to trust. I was looking for a new person like George.

Looking For Love

THE MAN OF HER DREAMS HAD A GOOD FRIEND AND I SUDDENLY found myself attracted and looking for a long-term relationship. He was ten years older than I was and everyone loved him and so did I too. One of his nicknames was Frank and he told me the name belonged to a famous gay man from the past. I would have chosen to call him 'Famous Frank' because to everyone we knew he was just cool. Frank was like the Pied Piper. The children in the group thought he was super cool.

We married and I saw a different person. I privately would have wanted to call him 'Furious Frank' or even 'Fearful Frank' because he was too private to talk about the past, his past and everything that had a past. I have decided that 'Fearful Frank' is a much better description. The best thing about Frank was that he was part of the group of people I loved most of all.

Of course, I never could tell 'Fearful Frank' about my past. Looking back, we ran a house full of secrets, silences, timetables, lies and loveless, painful encounters.

The man I married was not the man the friends knew and I'm sure the same would have been true for his workmates and his family. He told me that sex was a routine on Saturday nights preferably between 10 and 10.15pm.

There was no tenderness, no unnecessary touching, no kissing and no foreplay. There was o holding hands. There was no discussion and no chance to ever ask why.

All I ever knew was pain. It was both physical and emotional. What was wrong with me?

I never saw the way he treated me as evidence of anger. He had never wanted children and I was glad of that. I didn't think I could ever handle having a husband who found it necessary to touch up my toddler. It suited me. I would be scared for them the whole of their lives. I found that so terrifying. While I was always hurt by his remarks I didn't think I needed to change the subject or make my own case evident. On the other hand, I blamed myself for his attitude to fatherhood and his attitude towards me and intimacy. I had caused this. The problem was with me. It had to be me.

To think there was a different reason would have had me giving my life to a marvellous monster.

This was, after all, wasn't my reaction to Jerk coming back to haunt me it was because Frank was fixed on a different kind of **cringe** that involved silence, derision and rejection.

The coldness extended into other parts of my life as well. Sadly, Frank liked to lecture me on all manner of matters such as reliability, my ease in trusting people, my willingness to believe people when they said nice things about the dinner I had served or the party I organised.

All of this was piled on top of the insecurity I felt because I had a secret. I soon felt the same feelings of shame and unworthiness I had felt as a child. I was unclean and I was sure I deserved everything that was being dished out. I can now see that it was because of the criticism and put downs were just what I had experienced as a child. There was a small difference but it was hurtful and insensitive and very cruel because I wanted him to care for me.

After all this time, I have come to the sad realisation that once again I was victim of **furiousity**. It was **cringe** on ice.

In many ways it was even more deadly. I didn't deal with it while I was with him. I couldn't. I left. I was devastated. It took 15 years to make a move. I had heard it all before but this was someone who was supposed to love me.

One of the saddest things about **furiousity** is it really is best served icy cold by someone who cares about you and is vulnerable because they care. I forgot what I learned from George.

Frank was never somebody you could interrupt with humour or playfulness. He would become very angry and even more hurtful. He was much too damaged to accept intervention as anything but conflict and to try to interrupt him would have him resort to punishment by weeks and weeks of silence.

We didn't ever talk about our work, our other lives and interests or about our feelings. We only talked about the things we shared like replacing carpet, looking after pets and dealing with the traffic that made navigating the entrance to our home so perilous. Every other subject seemed out of bounds. And that was also stuff about my family and friends although I was to learn much later that there was so much more he could have told me about his family. When something good happened at work he didn't want to hear about it. He never told me about anything that happened at his workplace. Other people told me how clever and appreciated he was but I could not get much out of him. If I asked a question it would be answered with scorn. I think that I would describe myself as being always sad.

I would cry on the way to work as I drove along the freeway. I would feel sad on the way home. If a sad song played on the car radio I would start to cry and I would be a mess. Sometimes I would just sit at the side of the road waiting for the sadness to pass.

All the time, I thought it was me causing the problem. I had known sadness all my life and I just couldn't share it. It was my fault for not being enough for Frank. How could it be his fault? The blame must be here with me. Why did I think for a moment that it wasn't 'there'?

Not being able to concentrate on my important job I decided that I had to do something to change the way I was, I resigned and started a new business as a consultant. I found myself an office to work from and found that I didn't want to go home. A good friend offered me a bed-sit as she was moving in with her partner and it wasn't very long after that I left my marriage.

Frank wasn't angry and I felt sure that he was somewhat relieved. Have you noticed that I haven't been at all flippant when talking about my marriage? It was the hardest thing I have ever done in my life to break up and the way Frank took it just proved that the fault was here with me. I was so sure that he never knew I had been violated as a child. I had been so very careful not to leave any clues. But as wives go I had to be different. I was different. I didn't know how but I was failing marriage 101 and badly, very badly indeed. But how much of that was because my husband knew only **cringe** to communicate?

I did notice that there was a time that I wasn't sure whether I was in any danger. I wasn't afraid of Frank but I wondered why I wasn't. He seemed to be angry but afraid to show it. If he was upset at all he never spoke of it. I had told me he was a little embarrassed. I told him he could tell people I had discovered I was a lesbian. I knew I wasn't of course and he didn't do that.

I was determined not to fail Friends 101 principles and I am pleased to say that we stayed on good terms for years. I would later become his carer in the last year of his life when he died of that family 'awfulness illness'. Frank's family's deathly virus had seen many relatives cark it. I was to become aware that we had escaped a terrible fate and it would have quite likely been the same as the one suffered by Bro No2 who watched his children die one by one. The nature of the disease hasn't yet been uncovered. But there was another sinister reason that Frank didn't ever want to have children.

We had never shared our stories and if we had we would have realised why neither of us ever wanted to become parents. I would have realised why he was so cold and uncaring. I would have realised that as couples go we were perfectly matched for disaster.

Less than a year after I had left my marriage and moved to just around the corner from Frank's Bro No1, I was invited to the older brother's house to share his birthday cake.

I was ready for the good old talking-to as Bro No1 was a devout church attendee and I had promised to love, honour and obey his youngest brother in a Catholic ceremony no less. Bro 1 was a single man who went to mass at the City church every day. He was kind and a good friend to me. I would often eat out with him and some of his friends.

On the day as he shared his birthday cake he told me how three boys were left motherless after she was stricken with what was possibly, I was to realise later, the awful disease that was to kill Frank. Bro 1 told me that Frank was 3 years of age when the mother died so suddenly.

The other brothers were already at school and without their mother to look after them they were living with two aunts who had been nuns. Their father, a friendly postman was also chasing every six o'clock closing at pubs in the town and couldn't cope with both the loss of his wife and looking after three young boys. In a manner which will never be explained, the brothers and little Frank were handed over to two religious brothers from a local order. They offered to babysit the youngest and nobody seemed to ever ask what that meant and what went on in the years up until he started school.

All that Bro 1 would tell me was that Frank was frightened of them and would run away. He would come home for tea and the cycle would start all over again. He hinted at what happened to the older boys and I knew that they were interfered with as well. As he continued, the story got to be more revealing.

When Frank got older and he was sent off to school, he was

afraid of the teachers and some kind soul told him that the best way to escape their clutches was to be good at sport. He became Winning Frank and it worked. He couldn't stop playing sport and he couldn't stop winning. Even much later when he could no longer win he was unhappy and he was always very worried. All of this information came from my brother in-law. Only now can I see why the kind of **furiousity** that I met was of the icy cold and heartless kind. Frank had so much to be angry about and finally, he had someone he could serve it to.

I married a winner but I was left with a loser. We were both losers and none of it was our fault. The blame wasn't here with me after all. George would have been the first to agree. But George was not living in sharing distance. He was still in New South Wales and I knew how much I need him.

It is not hard to understand how Frank now having problems with his heart and not being able to play his beloved squash games was devastated. He took early retirement and painted the house five times. He disappeared into himself and it was really hard to be with him. After being told of the abuse he had suffered I kept seeing him as a small boy, a baby who was in no position to stop what happened. And, how much of the **cringe** was really a cry for help in the only way he knew how? Whatever was there when we first married was gone. There was no trust. I found that I couldn't share any of my joys, fears and aspirations with him. This was just like being sent to Coventry. Yes indeed it so much harder to deal with because it was all of that in what you could call **'cringe on steroids'.**

This explained so much to me. I realised that it would never have helped me to change the way he was but it certainly stopped me from being angry with him and angry with myself for marrying him in the first place.

My first reaction had been to blame the Church. Bro 1 showed me that the blame lay with the evil men who would use the background of a religious life to violate and abuse a small child. It wasn't the Church physically using his little body and destroying his future. It was the evil men who hid there all the time fouling the lives of so many. If I blamed anyone for what happened to Frank I would have to blame the aunts as they gave those bastards the means.

This was just as Lillian and George had accidentally done for Jerk. How much of that was just plain ignorance? If I blamed the Church it would be for turning a blind eye and for a world that would let the bastards off the hook when they should now be burning in hell.

Living With Mr. Cruel

All I could think of was how those people could ignore what was happening to that poor little boy. I had no pictures of him at that age but in my mind's eye I could see his fear and his tears. I don't know and will never know what they did to him. How could his aunts miss the clues? How could they not know his pain? I had a very angry husband. I do remembering him telling me once that he was afraid of his own temper. I never saw his temper. Yet that very kind man was so very cruel. Well that's **cringe**. I now know that to try and talk about it all with Frank would have served little purpose. I knew he would feel ashamed of what had been done to him. I knew he would have felt betrayed, rejected, used and abused. I know. We had been married in his church but I knew he didn't go to church. I arranged his funeral at his church because I knew that was what he would have wanted but that was about family tradition.

He was much loved. The people who came told me stories of the difference he has made in their lives. Oh how I wish I had known him that well. I then realised that the inner man, the person I would have been struggling to get to know was always going to hide from me because I might be able to see his pain.

At one time during his funeral, one of his oldest friends who I have never met before told me that he had advised Frank to never marry. I told him that I was burying a nice man who had to love me in the only way he knew how. We hugged and I have never seen or heard of that man again but I am sure he knew Frank's story. Frank and Lillian had hurt me in a different ways with their words. We had agreed to live apart but we were together in a very real sense for the last 12 months of his life. I could never have helped the pain of all of that to go away. I knew that. It would have just added to his pain to have shared mine.

I did the right thing by him and I know that he cared as much as he could. I was still really angry with him for tricking me into a marriage that could never have worked.

I know it was just because he wanted to be like everyone else. But who was I to judge? I had done the same thing. It was only after I stepped away from my marriage and no longer heard all the negative stuff that I remembered what my Dad taught me.

The comment about being a lesbian was one of those half serious, half joking, half heard remarks that were designed to avoid getting involved in a conversation and a debate I couldn't win.

I have heard so many stories of people who married and found they were unable to show love, to trust and so unable to talk about the past. Sometimes the person they married thought they could change them and make them happy. It doesn't work that way. When Perps have done their worst it's too late for anyone to make any sort of change. My husband was like that. Thanks to George I finally got to recognize what was happening to me. And thanks to Frank's brother I was able to put the pieces of the puzzle together. Other abused people just spend their lives in misery and are alone in a relationship in which the agony festers on forever. It was the secrets. I would often ask him why he was so angry. He would tell me that I had no right to delve into his personal story or ask questions about his family. His greetings would often be designed to put me in my place, to make me feel ill at ease and to start me worrying about what I had done to deserve his criticism. I was always on the back foot. If only I had known that being a serious interruption could have made a difference. The biggest thing I noticed after a time was that I had mistakenly married a man with no sense of humour and no gentleness. He always seemed to be so angry with me but he couldn't ever say why. That's why **'furiousity'** is such a great name for this.

For Frank, that was about the need to blot out the shame and the need to deal with the pain.

OMG! That's what **furiousity** is. It is not about something extra that is there in the person. It is about what is missing. Because they never had it they can never find a way to get it back.

Frank may have seemed at times to be amused but he never saw the funny side of anything when we were on our own. Imagine going through life always being angry or ready to be angry. I thought I made him angry. I didn't realise that he had been taught to be always and forever sad and angry after his mother died when he was just three years old.

I had a mother but she was ready to blame me for her unhappiness along with my father. Of course I know that the reason I got the treatment was not because she was jealous of my relationship with Jerk. It was because she saw that I trusted in Dad. I am sure that it was about my relationship with George that was keeping her angry. When he died many years later, my mother said, "**Perhaps now you will see my side of things**". I didn't of course.

I had not lived with George from the time I was seventeen and that was after Lillian tricked him into selling the house on the pretence that she would pack us all up and go to Sydney where Nice Nana, George's mother owned a terrace house in Woollahra. It was a neat trick and George fell for it. She managed to get rid of me at the same time and I only found out when I was on holiday and could not return to our Melbourne home. I moved into a flat with one of the girls from the Church I was attending.

I found solace and dare I say it, forgiveness, in the church group. But I never found anyone with whom I could share my story. I was too ashamed. But I did notice that there was never any **furiousity**. Nobody, it seems, had any need to pass on the hurt. I forgave myself.

It would be many years before I was again living with a less furious Lillian. My mother had rid herself of the deaf person who infuriated her. So that's why Lillian would seem at times to be amused but then turn on me and turn into an angry monster who only wanted to dish out the hurt and seemed to enjoy my discomfort and pain. I was older and wiser and I had learned well from George who stayed in New South Wales away from her poison and fury. If I wasn't tired I would spar with my mother. Most the time I would just turn on my heel and walk away. But I never trusted her. If you are into **cringe** you will never be trusted. I would have given anything to hear her say something like,

"***Well here's my lovely daughter***".

And what about my mother's mother, Nasty Nana? All the while, Nasty Nana thought she was such a great example of grace and decorum. This gave her the right to point out where I was a social failure. She was the one to remind me that I was a '**trollop**' and I blame her for a lot of my mother's rhetoric. I learned not to be nasty or cruel with Nasty Nana and I found that asking a complicated question was the best way to deal with her invective. Sometimes I wasn't quite ready for her attacks. It was never a pleasure to see her. Sometime she would simply refer to my looks and suggest that I was burning the candle at both ends. On those occasions I wouldn't even both to say anything at all. And then there was the poetry and the little references that would stop her dead in her tracks when she was on a **cringe** bender.

“Here’s To Little Miss Dirty Pants”

Nasty Nana’s great grandfather was rumoured to have been a constable from Somerset in the UK and I have no doubt that Nana thought it wrapped her in a cloak of respectability while all around the world festered and groaned covered with the sores of wickedness. She also believed that there was a curse waiting to get her and hers. When it first arrived, she decided that her whole life was turned upside down and nothing could have been worse than that. I would have never stood a chance in Hades of attracting her sympathy or even her understanding.

Not long before she died I presented Nasty Nana with another royal family poem after which she took my hand and said, **“I am so very sorry. I was very hard on you.”** I held her hand and she looked into my eyes with love for the very first time. That was huge. I comforted myself by concluding that my grandmother had been completely out of the loop and had very little chance to see that the way she was did nobody any good. All that time virtually alone on a farm at the top of the hill. That would turn anyone into a **cringe** machine.

It is hard to imagine a time when there was nothing technological invented or even dreamt of. Translate that as no machines or anything that would eventually be improved by Wi-Fi. When my mother was growing up there were no machines that I can think of that we are using today. Mowing machines were a herd of hungry goats. Milking machines were someone’s strong hands and arms and a stool that didn’t topple. Nobody thought of using machines to deliver words or pictures other than in a bound volume or via a news sheet. It was a time of messages delivered with smoke signals or with cow or church bells. A family knew the only way to be sure that their members were safe was to not let them out of the house. How things have changed. I tried very hard to put myself in her shoes and to take into account that most of the information Lillian got along the way was probably false and used to explain something that was not understood.

In that era, the only way to verify a story was to hear it at first hand or bear witness to some horrifying and terrible event. But while whispers could travel on the wind it seems getting it from the horses' mouth was not usually an option.

There may have been clunky old telephones but they weren't in the houses and they certainly weren't out in most country areas. There were no wearable devices designed for young people to tell the time or forecast the weather. Of course they worked out what the weather would be by looking at the clouds and watching to see if the cows started heading for the barn other than at milking time. The first news about an approaching bushfire was the smoke and fire running up the hill, sometimes just behind one of the farm workers and sometimes (actually always) destroying the washing. My Aunt told me that what I saw as **cringe** was just gossip repeated over and over again.

Rumours about fires lit in anger or due to gross stupidity set off up the hill at the same time. The man of the house might find a shilling or two and become the proud owner of a magnificent fob watch. Of course the rest of the family had to rely on something like the grandfather clock in the hall or the church clock if they were in town. For those who couldn't see the face of a clock, the bells or chimes had to do the job every hour.

Sometimes smoke was just your neighbour letting you know that Cousin Syd or Uncle Fergie were back from the latest horse sales and if it was Syd he would very likely have had a new mare to keep his old stallion 'Brutus' happy with his harem. Brutus would have sniffed her on the wind from miles away so there was no need to find a way to announce a homecoming. He would let them know by bellowing that the group was returning and the man of the house would be home for dinner within the hour. "***Someone fetch his slippers***". Nobody had really invented long distance phones. A man on a horse riding to your door would be likely to be there to tell you that the man of the house was at death's door having been sat on by a circus elephant or as a result of a vicious fight with a drunken competitor. Either would have been just as fatal.

Maybe your oldest child was in hospital having crashed an experimental hot air balloon or, maybe it was just time to collect census details again. Why do you think that neighbours were known to regularly gossip over the fence or at the bottom of the paddock? They exchanged information about who was dying, giving birth or arriving to help Pa with the new flock of experimental exotic sheep he was managing over the hill. Babies were born and welcomed into the household nine months after father's last trip. Babies were sometimes not registered especially if they had entered the world with two heads. Many of the stories people didn't want to get told were likely to spread on the wind. Rumours were rife but secrets stayed buried.

That was the silly world my mother knew. Is that why she had such a bad run with **cringe**? If some important person was involved in something nasty it was deemed necessary to cover it up especially if they had power and influence. I'm sure that my Perp was never going to do anything that would affect his reputation as an accountant. He would most certainly have covered all his bases and never let anyone suspect that he preferred to mess with little children. I am very sure that he had managed to convince Lillian that it would be only a matter of time until they waltzed off into the sunset together. This maybe explains how my mother depended on **cringe** and didn't think twice about the harm she was doing.

It was only when I thought how my mother came across and what she was like in her dealings with the family and the outside world that I saw that while she was very comfortable with being considered 'silly' she would never for a moment accept that she was foolish. But foolish and silly she was. She would have described her life as full and interesting. I think it was always dull and boring. I tried ballroom dancing and found it dull and boring. Some people dedicate their lives to it. Going to a room full of men you don't know and dancing only with the ones who ask you and probably fancy you. Now that's silly. There could be a Perp among them.

Please remember that while parents are being silly or behaving badly the Perp will know and be at it right under their noses. It's the chaos that they feed on. Any sort of sensational and scary news was avoided along with news of the suspicion that the local shopkeeper had been fiddling with the young daughter of the teacher and buying her silence with a bag of boiled lollies. Never! Would he? That could have been the curse once again. Young daughters out on their own were always likely to meet some foul play and it wasn't just being kicked by the milkman's horse. If you lived on the land and were a young, eligible woman who they knew was being molested you would know that very few marriage prospects would ever come to your door. Sometimes you just had to settle for the milkman even though his horse didn't like you.

The Christmas or Easter markets might be the place to show off your bosom and your ankles. If you were a single man of any age your past didn't matter.

Lillian would have known little about the devious ways of paedophiles and perverts. Mothers from miles around would send their sad daughters to the fairs to be checked over like a new milking cow. All women were expected to be buxom and fit but not too clever. She had to know how to cook, sew, maybe milk cows and had to look like she might be an asset to a man's bed and give him big, strong sons. She must never look like she was likely or ready to answer you back. Sometimes I wonder if most girls of the time were used to being molested.

Nobody had anything to say about the suitor's habits with child fiddling and that it was likely that he would end up doing to same to his own children. A suitor was judged by parents with a strange set of requirements and none of them took any notice of his sexual indications and foibles. Some young country girls had to follow their parents' wishes and take the bad with the good. Any young girl would have decided that if she hadn't developed all the right skills to enable her keep on top of the milking pile her bloody arms would fall off and who would want to put their hairy arms around her then? It explained a lot of angry and sad people. Lillian was a sad lady with a sad story.

As automatic backstop and future lady of the house, the oldest daughter should not contemplate marriage, any nookie or taking up holy orders. If your dad was always away toiling and having a good time it seems you would need to care for the woman who was your mother and was more often than not, someone who was extremely unhappy and often quite savage. They were the real slaves to the life in the bush. That was your lot unless you tried to escape. Sometimes, worn out, the young women would be out of there with the next travelling salesman armed with knickers, a good corset, winter nightgowns and strong vows that there would be no turning or looking back. Nobody asked if the travelling salesman had a reputation for de-flowering young women or sleeping with as many lonely farmer's wives as possible. On reflection, I would have been safer with one of those guys. On my reflection, I am very sure that I would never have been protected by Nasty Nana.

It is not at all hard to accept that Nasty Nana had started out as youngest daughter slowly watching her older siblings finding love or whatever and leaving the job of caring for grumpy parents to her. I can image that she was the one who longed to have graced the corridors of some stately home or lit up the floorboards as lead soprano in the state opera. Any of those ferocious mothers who were also known as 'those who rule the roost' were likely to turn their daughters into a Nasty Nana. I thought every family must have at least one Nasty Nana. I thought that somewhere in that maze of circumstances I would find the reason for the outbursts of **cringe** from my mother and my grandmother. If it was that excusable and that predictable we could expect to find it everywhere but we don't.

Cringe Is Taught

I hold that it is passed down through the generations by people who think they have to do it for reasons of discipline, respect for elders, their own self respect and their lack of respect for those they are supposed to nurture and care for. I decided that Nana was nasty because she had her own story that suggested she would have done well to escape when she was younger. It would never have occurred to me that she was one of the ones who escaped.

I don't know enough about her life before her marriage to offer it up as a reason for the way she was. We will never know what our great grandmother on our mother's side was like. Nasty Nana never shared any information like that. We only ever heard the bad stuff and why we were so bad ourselves. Surely there must have been a time when she was proud of her daughters.

Our Nasty Nana would have liked to have sent the troops after her girls I think. She needed them to help look after the farm because their dad was always away being a travelling salesman, in this case selling stock and property. The boys could do whatever they pleased. It would not have been at all kind to us to make us spend a lot of time with her. We always knew her to be one of the grumpiest people on earth.

Lillian stayed for as long as she could and that's where she learned the art of nastiness and above all, the art of survival and of ignoring anything unpleasant. My mother excelled in formidable womanhood mixed with being quite presentable and reliably well dressed. She was to me the perfect lady while she was being the ever complaining all-dancing chief cook and bottle washer. She may have been the gentlest youngest daughter trying to be so quick on her feet that should and one day could escape from Gippsland and a promising career as a long-time, full-time care-person for her getting elderly parents. She had to be better than her older sisters who had already shot through much to her dismay. Was her indifference perhaps her practicing the art of keeping quiet around what she saw as a strong man? She was always pleased to tell everyone that the older of the two was married to their neighbourhood drunk and sister number two was an old maid stuck in someone else's kitchen.

My mother felt sure she had been destined for greatness and all she had to do was run away from the person who dished the dirt. She packed her bags and all that **cringe** she had learned and set out to do her own thing.

When it had escaped her she was also very sure that our family line was cursed and it was her triumph to have escaped from everything that looked like the evil of servitude for an uncaring and spiteful mother. She had brought **cringe** with her and she was ready to use it.

If my Perp was a sleaze I would suspect that she thought he was being manly even though there was evidence that the curse of being a nonce had him by the balls. I was always too afraid to ask her how, what and where the curse she talked about had originated and how it was going to affect everyone. She would always attribute some misfortune or disaster to 'the curse'. She was sure she had plenty of proof. There were some very sad things that happened on her path to glory and I can now see it some success in her life meant it was easy for her to believe that she might be half right. She didn't know that there was no curse and all there really ever was sadly was, a huge amount of **furiousity** and **cringe**.

I decided that before I took my last breath I would endeavour to investigate the aforesaid curse and see if it still had some power over what happened to all of us. Was I a victim of the curse as I fought to avoid my assailant and was that all it was ever going to dish out to me?

Every time my mother, who claimed to be a little bit 'fey', read clairvoyant, got out the Ouija board she finished the exercise convinced that she had delivered a blow to apathy, the main tool of the curse. She was sure she was on top of it but each time it hit her she was left without a clue of how to get rid of the current version of it. I already knew about curse routines like not walking on the cracks, not following bears and not crossing behind a bus. One of my school friends told me never to meet the gaze of a pigeon.

My supposedly Fey Mum showed me an old leather covered photo album. I remember it because it was a dark maroon cover and when I asked her was the cover was made of she said it was from the hide of an animal. I didn't ask which animal but I was secretly bent on finding that creature with the maroon skin. The album was full mainly with pictures of a youthful Mum decked out in the latest fashion of the time. My boyish, sexy looking Dad appeared in some of the black and white snaps. The very last photo in the album was of my parents and me as a baby. Mum said I was in the arms of my paternal grandmother. It was not Nasty Nana. I looked very safe. I looked for the curse and it wasn't there.

The other Nana was never heard to say anything cruel or hurtful. How come that was possible?

There was never a photo of my mother's mother (Nasty Nana) that wasn't posing at court like she thought she should meet the Queen. I felt very sad for her at times.

It seemed to me that she would never be caught dead in a photo with an infant child. That would be like being photographed with a poddy calf. Ironically, unknown to my mother who was estranged at the time I was actually presented to royalty in the form of the Queen's cousin. True! I promise!

I am very sure that I kept these poems and sayings to hold on to the anger. Perhaps I thought I could share them with my sister. I really thought that my sister would have to forgive me one day. She didn't of course. We never settled our differences so it was a forlorn hope.

That's the guff on my mother and how I got through my childhood and my teens still being angry about what had happened to me. I didn't tell her. She didn't notice. I just wanted her to love me. I think I wanted her to forgive me but much later I wondered what for. My father was another matter.

Although he was gone for much of my life I remembered that he loved me. I do remember him as a bit of a philosopher. Is the story of **furiousity** in your family very much different?

While I was finding and getting a new appreciation once more of George I stumbled on some truths I feel are so worth sharing even if it's only to make me feel much better about how my life started and what happened along the way. Those truths are about

- ***recognizing cringe***
- ***switching to reject and defend mode***
- ***changing behaviour***
- ***living in a cringe-free world***

It would indeed be remiss of me if I didn't pass on to you the recipe for the removal of **cringe** in our lives. It serves no healthy purpose. It does nothing to help the target and, although they are unlikely to believe this, each time it is used it takes something profound away from the person who is making use of it. What if everybody practiced **cringe** removal? What if everybody took the pledge to eradicate it?

And what if observers could see how to alert others to the news that **cringe** is being tolerated?

In order to switch to reject and defend and change behaviour you will need to be on the alert. The first question to answer is **how to recognise it?** The elements to **cringe** talk are:

- Nothing is loving or approving
- Something derogatory was said
- Something derogatory was disguised as humour
- A hint of disapproval was in the greeting
- A hint of "I'm telling you or I told you so" was in the greeting
- The use of unfamiliar language or descriptors was obvious
- A type of sneer was evident
- An abundance of righteousness on the part of the speaker is evident
- Full frontal approach was obvious
- It was never whispered
- It was delivered with a faint giggle
- It was delivered with a raised voice
- A challenge was implied.

Sound familiar? **Cringe** ***is*** never light or chatty but can be if the perpetrator is particularly cruel.

To switch to reject or defend mode requires you to be ready for

- Clear thinking and intention to change the mood
- Going into switch off mode to have the target forget what was just said
- Delivering a trigger to restart the thought process
- Deep breaths

Intention comes when you hear something that tells you that **cringe** is in motion.

One of the most important things to do is to find a word to start the **switch off** process.

- One that I have learned to use is **OUCH!**

The **trigger** is based on what you want to convey. My advice is to never turn on the person who is delivering the **cringe** unless you are very sure of yourself. The very last thing that needs to happen is an argument with the person speaking.

If in doubt you can always use the old remedy

"**Are you OK**?"

I would prefer something like

"**Would you like a cuppa or a biscuit?**"

Some ideas for **triggers** would be

- Drawing attention to external noise or possible interruptions.
- Changing the subject completely with a tale like the one about the lady with the cat.
- Selecting one word they have said and going into an explanation of its meaning and day to day usage. For example "Did you know that the tart was actually invented in a bakery in the south of France? Is that the tart you are talking about?" I made that one up.
- Being an intervention by saying something like "Can we talk about this over a cuppa?"

Deep breaths are what you need after you realise that you just hit a home run. This is the time to erase what has been said from your mind. If you know that the perpetrator has had second thoughts you can acknowledge what just happened by saying something like

"Where were we?"

Remember that the perpetrator will do the **cringe** thing over and over again until they realise that they are not getting any traction or they realise what they have been saying actually hurts.. They will recognise your resistance by what they hear. It is so worth it for your own sake and because in most cases the person dishing it out usually thinks they have to be like that and that they are not doing anything wrong.

And now the most difficult task of all. The hardest intervention is when you hear **cringe** being used on a small child. What do you say without interfering to cause upset? There are a number of important rules.

- Don't try to explain or replace what was just said to the child.
- Change the subject in a flash
- Say something loving and comforting
- Turn to the **cringe speaker** and get them to agree to what you just said. If they won't you can say something that was quite different but still supportive of the child so that the child is left with something positive and comforting.

And most important

- Tell the perpetrator that you are on a pilgrimage to make children smile. Never deviate from that explanation because nobody can fault it.

One example might be
The **cringe** speaker says

"Here's the little monster"

The **cringe** fighter says

"The icecream monster. I love icecream."

Many of these sayings were created at a time when children had no access to images of monsters. If I had been faced with the idea that someone was a monster when I was growing up I would probably thought about one of those soldiers who came home with half a face, without any legs or with the effect of very bad burns. I can image that a child who was told they were a monster after the war ended would have been quite distressed.

Yet the labelling continues and we have no idea which child could be affected by being greeted that way. How can this use of **cringe** still be allowed to continue? Why can't the greetings be about love and affection? There are a number of rules you may be able to share with the people using **cringe talk** on children. They include:

- Monster see monster be
- When you share your love you share yourself
- Children are born without faults and they are not guilty
- A child that hears love will know love
- Children don't know about motives
- Take your anger out on a child and you have stolen a chunk of their lives
- Love your child and be loved in return
- Help them to love you and they will share

- Perps can't get a foothold in families where love and trust abounds
- You are responsible so don't make them wear your grief and anger

And if I was to say what I hold to be the most important actions they would be

- Be a serious interruption and show them they are safe
- Don't put anything off.

Can you imagine what a ***world without*** **cringe** would look like? How many children would be saved from unhappiness and pain? How many would be stronger and safer? What an exciting prospect? It is so worth doing.

My mother couldn't praise and encourage me and even if she could have there is no way that she would have given me the satisfaction. It wasn't at all unusual for her to say that I should know only what was good for me. I really think that was a Nasty Nana way of controlling people. Lillian was a good learner. When it came to dishing it out to George it would look like

"Man of the house, less hero, more mouse."

She knew how to keep others out of the loop. It is not such a surprise that for most of my life I have been involved in work that involved looking at how information is made available, how it is withheld and what happens when the information or the manner in which it is dispensed does not suit the intended target.

Make sharing love be the game.

I have seen examples where there is so much information but its volume hides the detail, sense and purpose and the intended target ends up none the wiser. There may be times when that is life threatening. There may be times when that obfuscation is quite deliberate. When George went to hospital with the lump in his testicle we were told that he was having an operation on his ears. Lillian would never have been caught using the word 'testicle". She would get very upset if we ever said the word 'sex'. No smut in her world. There was only **cringe** and the need to call her daughter all kinds of prostitute. That does not compute.

I thought that our family was the only one that ever had secrets. One way of keeping secrets was to stop ever mentioning certain people. If they were out of sight and out of mind nobody could speak ill of the rest of us.

When George was out of our sight it was as if he didn't exist. I would be in all sorts of trouble if I tried to say anything good about him. I now realize that Nasty Nana kept that way of keeping secrets going and had she been alive today she would never tolerate anybody looking for information about their ancestors. I think she would have had one of us take a packed lunch and a can of kerosene and head off to burn down an office belonging to ancestry and heritage sleuths. She must have been so terribly ashamed of her past. Wait on! That didn't match with royalty stories did it? Obfuscation!

Another way that Lillian could manage to deal with family secrets was to deliberately forget. Her ability to forget knew no bounds. That really helped her to dish out the dirt. I knew how much she blamed George for everything and I had that deep down feeling that she would turn on me. And of course she knew how to twist the truth so that my father's grandmother was transformed from being the matron of a women's hospital to a backyard abortionist.

Why did she need to do that? Later I was to reach the conclusion that my mother was always looking for a reason to be hateful and hurtful and making up stories about George's parents and grandparents made it easier for her to keep up the rage and dish out the dirt. None of us knew anything about our Dad's forefathers to be able to argue with her. Pop told us they were good folks.

I think back to Frank and his brutal loss of innocence. He deserved to be hugged but not by a predator. I see the zest for life in a little boy too young to understand what losing his mother would mean and too young to stand up for his rights after his Perps took over. What you don't see in this picture is the future he was going to have to bear all because there were those who would most assuredly claim that they were ever so gentle.

Now tell me that is not violence and in every sense of the word, destructive. Murderers can kill people with less violence. Frank wasn't always sad, angry, suspicious, scared and without hope.

I wasn't around to see Frank destroyed by those deviants but I was around to see the results of their evil activities. The man I thought I had entered into a partnership with didn't know how to really love and be loved. This kind of violence destroys the soul and steals a person's identity transforming them into someone who is angry and aggressive or fearful and timid for the rest of their lives. I would argue that most of the sexually abused never get help. There are no bruises, no broken limbs and no black eyes. Abusers of little children fiddle with the bodies of their victims but the really injury is with the soul and that remains hidden with the guilt and shame that was so bad.

I correct that. I remember that I had a black eye from the day he injured me in the chook house and I was bleeding quite a bit. When we arrived home Lillian gave me a lump of meat to try to relieve the pain. That was after Jerk claimed that I had fallen over and hit my head. I made up my mind there and then that the meat thing on the black eye didn't work. If my memory is correct it was a lump of sausage mince. Silly Lillian!

A child's life can be ruined with just one senseless act. It can be the stuff of nightmares. Even one senseless act is bad enough but what if it is regular liked clockwork. The longer it remains festering away in their psyche the longer it affects their personality, confidence and general mental health. It still upsets me that a little Frank aged 3 could be almost offered up to be hurt by some monsters and I know that he was starting off his life being so scared. We will never know what they did to him. His brothers knew but after school they would go to the mail centre where he worked as a postman and then wait outside the pub until after 6 when they would accompany their father as he staggered home.

What is even worse is that there is some sort of enquiry and someone is convicted and society breathes a sigh of relief very sure that they have it covered. For each child molester unmasked how many others go Scot free knowing that they will most certainly do it again. They will never seek help and always put themselves into situations where they can easily re-offend.

And of course it is not only men who offend. But what if it is catching?

I seriously used to wonder if I could become a Perp myself. It was a topic that I didn't understand and of course when I was growing up there was little media and I was never in danger of becoming interested in anything at all pornographic. My dear friend Flo thought it very funny to sing ditties in which she was substitute naughty words and I would put my fingers in my ears in mock horror. I could never tell her how they worried me. Would I become a deviant? Much later I realised that the guilt and the fear had stayed with me until I became an adult and after I joined the Church group.

There is nothing gentle about being forced to take part in a sex act no matter how old you might be. To me as a small child it was brutal. There is nothing that could have been done to that little boy that could have been called natural. It must have been ever so brutal. Who could he turn to? His aunts were never going to accept that anything bad was happening. The Frank I knew was a good and decent man but lost forever to anyone who would want to love him.

As for us! After sixteen years of marriage I had realised that nothing I did would change anything for him.

> I left today.
> I took my life and went away.
> Some of me is here, there and everywhere.
> I could go back.
> Go back to where I felt such pain
> And leave again.

When you bring children into the world don't you want them to be happy, find happiness with a partner and have children who will become an integral part of your life? If some grotesque Perp has found their way into your life and your family that will never happen. Don't ignore the elephant in the room. It just may be boring a hole in your life and trampling on your future happiness.

Of course it is about dealing with guilt and the feeling that you can't ever fail. If it was about dealing with the problem of the Perps that slide into our lives the ignorance and then saying that there's nothing wrong can be devastating. The part of this book that follows considers how the child, the teen and the adult is encouraged to do nothing, say nothing, feel nothing and hide everything.

Sad to say, George left our city and went to live with Nice Nana. He looked after her until she died. With Lillian's constant referral to dad as a man who never ever loved his family I was stricken with the thought that there was always something wrong. I always felt that I was on notice about something. I had written a poem about being under scrutiny.

I later realised that this poem was about the feelings I had as a child.

> There's someone sitting in my tree.
> He's sitting there just watching me.
> He watches every move I make and waits for every
> bad mistake.
> I'll turn around and meet his stare
> Oh goodness me! There's no-one there.

The day I wrote that I had a huge breakthrough. I was innocent.

After looking at the poem once again I have not too long ago realised that the person in the tree has always been a man. I wonder who! That's when I realised that in my young confused mind my abuser was also my judge and jury. Now that the bastard Jerk is dead I have no chance of ever confronting him and asking him to explain. When I was that small and vulnerable child there was so much to be explained but it never was. I do hope he is in Hell.

If my Dad was here today he would be telling me to write to anyone in charge of little children and tell them to:

- Stop being selfish;
- Know your children and what makes them happy, sad, angry, confused, and worried;
- Know the caregivers and watch the way that your child reacts to and with them;
- Supervise their online activities and use all the devices available now and in the future to stop their abuse and exploitation online;
- Educate yourself about the dangers of paedophilia;
- Rely on the professionals to decide if your child is in peril;

- Talk to your friends and share what you have learned about the subject;
- Love your child and be their friend;
- Don't be a bloody sceptic;
- Trust your child and believe their stories;
- If you can't take care of all the above – don't have children or take on responsibility of caring for them.

I have no doubt he would be saying

"Hold them tight and love them always".

I would like to think that the life I lived was able to compensate for what I know I must have lost. I am sad for Lillian, for my troubled sister, for lovely Frank and for all the little children who met a Perp along the way. It's not too late to do more. You can do more. Wake up to something's wrong as soon as it appears.

Of course, the good news is that paedophilia is rare and most people are safe with your children.

But being affected by **cringe** and forming bad feelings about themselves as they try to deal with issues that they don't understand or appreciate is another matter. The most worrying of these is when someone reinforces over and over again a description of that person that suggests they are not what you know them to be. I think that the worst thing about my Nasty Nana was that she would seem to accuse me of being dishonest and untrustworthy. I never knew why. I do know that it zapped my confidence and to hear her say,

"Well here comes our little story teller."

That was more than a little disarming. The only storytellers I knew were liars and cheats. I was later to learn that I really did like making up stories and looking back I wondered if she had that right all along. Nobody ever explained at the time. It didn't occur to me that she saw my need to write poems and share them as storytelling.

That connection was something that might have been revealed by my mother but she didn't see that I could be taking it the wrong way. All she would have needed to do was to call me **"Our little poet".**

I am very sure that George would have responded like that had he heard Nasty Nana's greeting. I do know that Nasty Nana must have learnt her **sexist** approach to **cringe** from somewhere.

Was it her forebears? She was only ever heard to say nice things about her sons but would let fly when it came to her approach to her three daughters.

Was it just her need to make sure that her daughters lived a clean and respectable life? I think not. She was more likely to treat them and accuse them as though they already lived a life of debauchery and shame.

She had so much respect for my mother that she stood across the road from the church where Lillian and George were married. One of the ways that Nasty Nana greeted us as a group was to refer to us as 'spawn of the devil'. She was talking about George of course because she was one of the people who expressed their concern that he was lying about his hearing loss. I realised as I got older that there were some people who were unwilling to see that someone had a disability preferring to believe that they were cowards or someone who would use it as an excuse to not play by the rules.

It is this kind of backgrounding that sets a person up to be prejudiced against a group who they think are playing a part in order to get some sort of benefit. There was never any way that George could have proved his deafness unless he was trying to register to go to war. Even then they refused to believe him. 'They' being mother and her mother.

- **Bigotry** is learnt and not inherited.
- **Sexism** is learnt and not inherited
- **Racism** is learnt and not inherited
- **Class intolerance** is learnt and not inherited
- **Homophobia** is learnt and not inherited
- **Religious intolerance** is learnt and not inherited
- **Xenophobia** or fear of strangers is learned and not inherited
- **Ageism** or attitudes towards the aged are learned and not inherited
- **Nationalism** of the fervent and violent kind is learned and not inherited.

I can't offer any interventions that George might have made in each of these areas. I do know that when someone said something about our aborigines he would say,

"They walked the earth long before our ancestors ever set sail."

George would have said that long before our Prime Minister Rudd made the famous apology to the stolen generation. That was all about respect. Before that, it would have been normal to hear someone deliver **cringe** with racism in tow. It is not hard to imagine that it still happens because of what some of us have been taught by our relatives. It has to stop. Now we have proof that our first nation peoples may have been the oldest races in the world and of course it has to stop.

Sometimes we hear someone refer to an older person as

"the old boy or the old lady"

or things worse than that and they say it to their face. How it lands sounds very much like "**fool".**

They may never say, "**Silly young fool"** or anything like that but it is so easy to say that about seniors.

What does that do for the respect we should be showing for the older generation? They were the ones who invented drugs to make us well, who fought wars to keep us safe, who designed cities and buildings in which we could live and work and were the first to come up with the ideas for new technology and they worked out how to write the software to fly planes, run businesses and banks and keep our cites lit for us at night. It's time to stop the **cringe**.

George would have said

"That older person will have forgotten more than you'll ever learn Buster"

And then there was **homophobic cringe**,

George would have asked someone who was being homophobic did they ever get a kick out of playing dressups. That was because he was of a generation that didn't understand that sexual preference was more biological than cultural. I do know that he would never have tolerated someone being bullied or terrorized because of it. He would never be heard to say something like

"Here is our favourite Butch lady."

I have heard that said to our boarder, Miss O just because she was still single.

Do Get A Grip On Yourself

I can't tell you how many times I have heard those words when faced with some upset, trauma or grief.

I would never say that to anyone. I would never feel that I was doing anyone any favours because these words seem to turn the trials of that person back onto themselves. It is just another way of saying that the targets of the words are hopeless and shouldn't ever complain or stand up for themselves. It is an underhand way of calling someone a liar. I hate the fact that the person who reverts to these tactics is often the person who has the most influence in the life of the person in trouble. In my case that person is usually a member of my family or sadly, at times, a supposedly well meaning friend. Sometimes it is a person who heard it themselves all of their lives and it seems has said it without much thought about others for the whole of their lives anyway.

And in their minds it always works. That kind of response would have the effect of having their friend or family member never sharing at all. That's what the Perps always counted on.

It's is often a way of covering the fact that the person who was confided in doesn't have a hope in Hades of saying anything that will help. In the context of this story it is also a way of avoiding the topic. It is a way of pushing matters to one side and dumping responsibility back on the victim. It's another way of saying "How dare you share your woes with me?" I know I never heard George say anything like that. There are a number of sayings designed to make us stop with the unpleasant stuff and they include:

"Get your act together."
"Nobody wants to hear your tales of woe."
"You're always winging about something or nothing at all."
(In my case: "Just like your father").
"Go tell it to the trees. They'll listen. They won't bark." (Ha Ha).
"Other people have enough troubles of their own."
"Somebody has put too many strange ideas in that head of yours."
"What pictures are you seeing on Saturday afternoons?"
"Stop always being in your head".
"I didn't bring you up to say hurtful things about other people."
"I would never let anyone do anything bad to you."
"It's just part of growing up. Grow up!"

And finally, the most used sayings from Lillian and family members:

"Stop dwelling on it".
"Just get on with your life and stop worrying about things you can't fix".
"Nobody wants to hear you moaning".
"We both know you probably imagined it all."

How old was I when I started hearing those things? Try five or six. Not even seven. I have heard it all my life. I always knew what would be said if I dared to speak up. I have heard much of it again recently and it made me so sad. I suddenly realized that it was actually verbal bullying.

Of course, most bullying is verbal and could it be that it all begins with learning to deliver **cringe**?

Then there is the opposite. When Frank was having a bad time with his health after we were separated I asked a family member to look in on him. He didn't say he wouldn't and I trusted him to reach out. He never told me that he never did. Before the separation they had been great mates. To pretend that a person will help and then do nothing is very cruel.

That's yet another way that people can abuse the abused. They promise to make contact with someone in authority on their behalf and they never do it. It could have stopped the Perp dead in their tracks but they did nothing. In my book that's being complicit.

Getting shunned was devastating. Even when I left primary school and went to high school I was sure that they all would know about me and I would wait for it to be announced at school assembly. It used to make me physically sick and I would spend a lot of time in the sick bay. Nobody said anything to me at high school but it was a select school where a few kids from each school got to attend. At primary school I was always waiting for kids to tell me I was rude, weird, a dirty mouth, nasty, horrible. It happened a few times but that was enough to make me afraid. These were the names I feared and that I still remember. There were many more. Jerk was dead but he haunted me every day. I really didn't know any other way than to shut my mouth completely. I used to walk along the street listening to adults talking and wondering if they were talking about their secrets. Surely everyone had their special secrets. I couldn't deal with the fact that maybe I was the only one.

I was never afraid at the Church most of the time and I felt very safe because I wasn't expected to tell all. But still I was terrified that someone would find out and finding Jerk's niece there was such a shock. I was so thankful that I was not asked to confess in the Congregational Church.

Hilda, the angry sister didn't have anything to do with the Church and my friends were not known to her. I am very sure she would have said something to spoil everything for me. She could be very bitter.

I mention all of this because I want people to know how hurtful and destructive they can be. Sometimes they are just repeating all the hurtful things that might have been said to them as they grew up. Not one of those sayings mentioned earlier does anything positive. They are no help at all and could be some of the triggers for someone taking some action to bring an end to it. Some of these are the kind of thing that a teacher might say. How cruel and thoughtless can they be?

How many times have you heard the comments made earlier said to a child? Who has the right to do that? Nobody has!

And then they wonder why the child becomes withdrawn, unhappy and sad. That's verbal abuse. Knowing now that this is what people do to the child that has been abused by some deviant why would you continue to abuse any child that way?

> It's up to you. I can only tell you what happened to me.
> Go lively! Keep them safe! Stay vigilant!
> Stay connected! Spread the love!
> Make sure they can hold on to their innocence!
> Take notice!
> Be able to say with love and confidence of **furiousity**
> and **cringe**

"IT ISN'T HERE"

CPSIA information can be obtained
at www.ICGtesting.com
Printed in the USA
LVHW050320090322
713001LV00009B/432

9 781982 292799